An Introduction to Zen Buddhism

An Introduction to

Zen Buddhism

D. T. Suzuki

Foreword by C. G. Jung

WAKING LION PRESS

ISBN 978-1-4341-0476-2

Published by Waking Lion Press, an imprint of the Editorium, LLC.

Waking Lion Press™ and Editorium™ are trademarks of:

The Editorium, LLC
West Jordan, UT 84081-6132
www.editorium.com

CONTENTS

PREFACE

THE articles collected here were originally written for the *New East*, which was published in Japan during the 1914 War under the editorship of Mr. Robertson Scott. The editor suggested publishing them in book-form, but I did not feel like doing so at that time. Later, they were made the basis of the First Series of my *Zen Essays* (1927), which, therefore, naturally cover more or less the same ground.

Recently, the idea came to me that the old papers might be after all reprinted in book-form. The reason is that my *Zen Essays* is too heavy for those who wish to have just a little preliminary knowledge of Zen. Will not, therefore, what may be regarded as an introductory work be welcomed by some of my foreign friends?

With this in view I have gone over the entire MS., and whatever inaccuracies I have come across in regard to diction as well as the material used have been corrected. While there are quite a few points I would like to see now expressed somewhat differently, I have left them as they stand, because their revision inevitably involves the recasting of the entire context. So long as they are not misrepresenting, they may remain as they were written.

If the book really serves as a sort of introduction to Zen Buddhism, and leads the reader up to the study of my other works, the object is attained. No claim is made here for a scholarly treatment of the subject-matter.

The companion book, *Manual of Zen Buddhism*, is recommended to be used with this *Introduction*.

D. T. S.

Kamakura, August 1934

FOREWORD

by Dr. C. G. Jung

DAISETZ TEITARO SUZUKI's works on Zen Buddhism are among the best contributions to the knowledge of living Buddhism that recent decades have produced, and Zen itself is the most important fruit that has sprung from that tree whose roots are the collections of the Pali-Canon.[1] We cannot be sufficiently grateful to the author, first for the fact of his having brought Zen closer to Western understanding, and secondly for the manner in which he has achieved this task. Oriental religious conceptions are usually so very different from our Western ones that even the very translation of the words brings one up against the greatest difficulties, quite apart from the meaning of the ideas exposed, which under certain circumstances are better left untranslated. I have only to mention the Chinese "*Tao*", which no European translation has yet achieved. The original Buddhist writings themselves contain views and ideas which are more or less unassimilable by the average Western understanding. I do not know, for example, just what spiritual (or perhaps climatic?) background or preparation is necessary before one can deduce any completely clear idea from the Buddhist *Kamma*. In spite of all that we know about the essence of Zen, here too there is the question of a central perception of unsurpassed singularity. This strange perception is called *Satori*, and may be translated as "Enlightenment". Suzuki says (see page 95), "*Satori* is the *raison d'être* of Zen, and without it there is no Zen." It should not be too difficult for the Western mind to grasp what a mystic understands by "enlightenment", or what is known as "enlightenment" in religious parlance.

[1] The origin, as Oriental authors themselves admit, is the "Flower Sermon" of Buddha. On this occasion he held up a flower to a gathering of students, without uttering a word. Only Kasyapa understood him. (Shuej Ohasama: *Zen. Der lebendige Buddhismus in Japan*, 1925, p. 3.)

9

Satori, however, depicts an art and a way of enlightenment which is practically impossible for the European to appreciate. I would point out the enlightenment of Hyakujo (Pai-chang Huai-hai, A.D. 724–814) on page 89, and the legend on pages 92–3 of this book.

The following may serve as a further example: A monk once went to Gensha, and wanted to learn where the entrance to the path of truth was. Gensha asked him, "Do you hear the murmuring of the brook?" "Yes, I hear it," answered the monk. "There is the entrance," the master instructed him.

I will be content with these few examples, which illustrate clearly the opacity of the *satori* experiences. Even if we take example after example, it is still extremely hazy how such an enlightenment comes and of what it consists; in other words, by what or about what one is enlightened. Kaiten Nukariya, who was himself a Professor at the So-To-Shu Buddhist College in Tokyo,[1] says, speaking of enlightenment:

"Having set ourselves free from the misconception of Self, next we must awaken our innermost wisdom, pure and divine, called the Mind of Buddha, or Bodhi, or Prajna by Zen Masters. It is the divine light, the inner heaven, the key to all moral treasures, the source of all influence and power, the seat of kindness, justice, sympathy, impartial love, humanity, and mercy, the measure of all things. When this innermost wisdom is fully awakened, we are able to realize that each and every one of us is identical in spirit, in essence, in nature with the universal life or Buddha, that each ever lives face to face with Buddha, that each is beset by the abundant grace of the Blessed One, that He arouses his moral nature, that He opens his spiritual eyes, that He unfolds his new capacity, that He appoints his mission, and that life is not an ocean of birth, disease, old age and death, nor the vale of tears, but the holy temple of Buddha, the Pure Land, where he can enjoy the bliss of Nirvana.

Then our minds go through an entire revolution. We are

[1] See his book: *The Religion of the Samurai*, 1913, p. 133.

no more troubled by anger and hatred, no more bitten by envy and ambition, no more stung by sorrow and chagrin, no more overwhelmed by melancholy and despair," etc.

That is how an Oriental, himself a disciple of Zen, describes the essence of enlightenment. It must be admitted that this passage would need only the most minute alterations in order not to be out of place in any Christian mystical book of devotion. Yet somehow it fails to help us as regards understanding the *satori* experience described by this all-embracing casuistry. Presumably Nukariya is speaking to Western rationalism, of which he himself has acquired a good dose, and that is why it all sounds so flatly edifying. The abstruse obscurity of the Zen anecdotes is preferable to this adaptation: *ad usum Delphini*; it conveys a great deal more, while saying less.

Zen is anything but a philosophy in the Western sense of the word.[1] This is the opinion expressed by Rudolf Otto in his introduction to Ohasama's book on *Zen*, when he says that Nukariya has fitted the magic oriental world of ideas into our Western philosophic categories, and confused it with these. If psycho-physical parallelism, the most wooden of all doctrines, is invoked in order to explain this mystical intuition of Not-twoness (*Nichtzweiheit*) and Oneness and the *coincidentia oppositorium*, one is completely ejected from the sphere of *koan* and *kwatsu* and *satori*.[2] It is far better to allow oneself to become deeply imbued beforehand with the exotic obscurity of the Zen anecdotes, and to bear in mind the whole time that *satori* is a *mysterium ineffabile*, as indeed the Zen masters wish it to be. Between the anecdotes and the mystical enlightenment there is, for our understanding, a gulf, the possibility of bridging which can at best be indicated but never in practice achieved.[3] One has the feeling of touching upon a true secret, not something that has been imagined or pretended; this is not a case of mystifying secrecy, but rather of

[1] "Zen is neither psychology nor philosophy."
[2] Otto in Ohasama: *Zen*, p. viii.
[3] If in spite of this I attempt "explanations" in what follows, I am still fully aware that in the sense of *satori* what I say can only be useless. I could not resist, however, the attempt to manœuvre our Western understanding at least into the proximity of an understanding—a task so difficult that in so doing one must take upon oneself certain crimes against the spirit of Zen.

an experience that baffles all languages. *Satori* comes as something unexpected, not to be expected.

When within the realm of Christianity visions of the Holy Trinity, the Madonna, the Crucifixion or the Patron Saint are vouchsafed, one has the impression that this is more or less as it should be. That Jacob Boehme should obtain a glimpse into the *centrum naturae* by means of the sunbeam reflected in the tin plate is also understandable. It is harder to accept Master Eckehart's vision of "the little naked boy",[1] or even Swedenborg's "man in the red coat" who wanted to wean him from overeating, and whom, in spite of this or perhaps because of it, he recognized as the Lord God.[2] Such things are difficult to accept, bordering as they do on the grotesque. Many of the *satori* experiences, however, do not merely border on the grotesque; they are right there in the midst of it, sounding like complete nonsense.

For anyone, however, who has devoted considerable time to studying with loving and understanding care the flowerlike nature of the spirit of the Far East, many of these amazing things, which drive the all too simple European from one perplexity to another, fall away. Zen is indeed one of the most wonderful blossoms of the Chinese spirit,[3] which was readily impregnated by the immense thought-world of Buddhism. He, therefore, who has really tried to understand Buddhist doctrine, if only to a certain degree—i.e. by renouncing various Western prejudices—will come upon certain depths beneath the bizarre cloak of the individual *satori* experiences, or will sense disquieting difficulties which the philosophic and religious West has up to now thought fit to disregard. As a philosopher, one is exclusively concerned with that understanding which, for its own part, has nothing to do with life. And as a Christian, one has nothing to do with paganism ("I thank thee, Lord, that I am not as other men"). There is no *satori* within these Western bounds—that is an Oriental affair. But is it really so? Have we in fact no *satori*?

[1] See *Texte aus der deutschen Mystik des 14 und 15, Jahrhunderts*, published by Adolf Spamer, 1912, p. 143.

[2] William White: *Emanuel Swedenborg*, 1867, Vol. I, p. 243.

[3] "Zen is undoubtedly one of the most precious and in many respects one of the most remarkable spiritual graces with which Oriental man has been blessed." (Suzuki: *Essays*, I, p. 249.)

When one examines the Zen text attentively, one cannot escape the impression that, with all that is bizarre in it, *satori* is, in fact, a matter of *natural occurrence*, of something so very simple[1] that one fails to see the wood for the trees, and in attempting to explain it, invariably says the very thing that drives others into the greatest confusion. Nukariya[2] therefore is right when he says that any attempt to explain or analyse the contents of Zen with regard to enlightenment would be in vain. Nevertheless, this author does venture to say of enlightenment that it embraces an *insight into the nature of self*, and that it is an emancipation of the conscious from an illusionary conception of self.[3] The illusion regarding the nature of self is the common confusion of the ego with self. Nukariya understands by "self" the All-Buddha, i.e. simply a total consciousness (*Bewusstsein-stotalität*) of life. He quotes Pan Shan, who says, "The world of the mind encloses the whole universe in its light," adding, "It is a cosmic life and a cosmic spirit, and at the same time an individual life and an individual spirit."[4]

However one may define self, it is always something other than the ego, and inasmuch as a higher understanding of the ego leads on to self the latter is a thing of wider scope, embracing the knowledge of the ego and therefore surpassing it. In the same way as the *ego* is a certain knowledge of my *self*, so is the self a knowledge of my ego, which, however, is no longer experienced in the form of a broader or higher ego, but in the form of a non-ego (*Nicht-Ich*).

Such thoughts are also familiar to the author of *Deutsche Theologie*[5]: "Any creature who is to become conscious of this perfection must first lose all creaturelikeness (*Geschopfesart*), something-ness (*Etwasheit*) and self." If I take any good to my-

---

[1] A master says: "Before a man studies Zen, mountains are mountains to him, and waters are waters. But when he obtains a glimpse into the truth of Zen through the instruction of a good master, mountains are no longer mountains, nor waters waters; later, however, when he has really reached the place of Rest (i.e. has attained *satori*), mountains are again mountains, and waters waters." (Suzuki: *Essays*, I, p. 12.)

[2] *Religion of the Samurai*, p. 123.

[3] "Enlightenment includes an insight into the nature of self. It is a liberation of the mind from deception regarding self."

[4] L.c. p. 132.

[5] *Das Buchlein vom vollkommen Leben.* Published by H. Buttner, 1907.

self, that comes from the delusion that it is mine, or that I am Good. That is always a sign of imperfection and folly. Were I conscious of the *truth*, I would also be aware that I am not Good, that Good is not mine and is not of me." "Man says, 'Poor fool that I am, I was under the delusion that I was it, but I find it *is* and *was* truly God'."

That already states a considerable amount regarding the contents of enlightenment. The occurrence of *satori* is interpreted and formulated as a break-through of a consciousness limited to the ego-form in the form of the non-ego-like self. This conception answers to the nature of Zen, but also to the mysticism of Master Eckehart.[1] The master says, in his sermon on "Blessed are the poor in spirit": "When I came out from God, all things said, 'There is a God!' But that cannot make me blissful, for with it I conceive myself to be a creature. But in the break-through,[2] when I wish to remain empty in the will of God, and empty also of this will of God and of all his works, and of God himself—then I am more than all creatures, for I am neither God nor creature: *I am what I am, and what I will remain*, now and forever! Then I receive a jerk, which raises me above all the angels. In this jerk I become so rich that God cannot suffice me, in spite of all that he is as God, in spite of all his Godly works; for in this break-through I perceive what God and I are in common. *I am then what I was*,[3] I grow neither less nor more, for I am an immovable being who moves all things. Here God no longer abides in man, for man through his poverty has won back what he has always been and will always be."

Here the master is actually describing a *satori* experience, a release of the ego through self, to which "Buddha-Nature", or godly universality, is added. Since, out of scientific modesty, I do not here presume to make any metaphysical declaration, but mean a change of consciousness that can be experienced,

---

[1] *Meister Eckehart's Schriften und Predigten*. Published by H. Buttner, 1912.

[2] There is a similar image in Zen: when a master was asked of what Buddhahood consisted, he answered, "The bottom of a pitcher is broken through." (Suzuki: *Essays in Zen Buddhism*, I, p. 217.) Another analogy is the "bursting open of the sack". (Suzuki: *Essays in Zen Buddhism*, II, p. 100.)

[3] Cf. Suzuki: *Essays in Zen Buddhism*, pp. 220, 241. Zen signifies a glimpse into the original nature of mankind, or the recognition of original man. (See also p. 144.)

I treat *satori* first of all as a psychological problem. For anyone who does not share or understand this point of view, the "explanation" will consist of nothing but words which have no tangible meaning for him. He is not then able to make of these abstractions a bridge to the facts related; in other words, he cannot understand how the perfume of the blossoming laurel (p. 90-1) or the tweaked nose (p. 87) should effect such a considerable change of consciousness. The simplest thing would be, of course, to relegate all these anecdotes to the realm of amusing fairy stories, or at least, if one accepts the facts as they are, to dispose of them as instances of self-deception. (One would also willingly use here the expression "auto-suggestion", that pathetic white elephant from the store of spiritual inadequacies!) A serious and responsible examination of the strange phenomena cannot lightly pass over these facts. We can of course never decide definitely whether a person is *really* "enlightened" or "redeemed", or whether he merely imagines it. We have no criteria for this. Moreover, we know well enough that an imaginary pain is often far more painful than a so-called real one, in that it is accompanied by a subtle moral suffering caused by the gloomy feeling of secret self-accusation. It is not, therefore, a question of "actual fact" but of *spiritual reality*; that is to say, the psychic occurrence of the happening known as *satori*.

Every spiritual happening is a picture and an imagination; were this not so, there could be no consciousness and no phenomenality of the occurrence. The imagination itself is a psychic occurrence, and therefore whether an "enlightenment" is called "real" or "imaginary" is quite immaterial. The man who has enlightenment, or alleges that he has it, thinks in any case that he is enlightened. What others think about it can determine nothing whatever for him with regard to his experience. Even if he were to lie, his lie would be a spiritual fact. Yes, even if all religious reports were nothing but conscious inventions and falsifications, a very interesting psychological treatise could still be written on the fact of such lies, with the same scientific treatment with which the psychopathology of delusions is presented. The fact that there is a religious movement upon which many brilliant minds have worked over a period of many centuries is sufficient reason for venturing at least upon a serious attempt to bring such happenings within the realm of scientific understanding.

Earlier on I raised the question of whether we have anything like *satori* in the West. If we except the sayings of our Western mystics, a superficial glance discloses nothing that could be likened to it in even the faintest degree. According to our thinking, the possibility that there are steps in the development of consciousness does not exist. The mere thought that there is a tremendous psychological difference between the consciousness of the existence of an object and the *"consciousness of the consciousness"* of an object borders on a subtlety which can scarcely be answered. One could hardly bring oneself to take such a problem so seriously as to take account of the psychological conditions of the setting of any such problem. It is characteristic that the posing of such and similar questions does not as a rule arise from any intellectual need, but where it exists is nearly always rooted in a primitive religious practice. In India it was Yoga and in China Buddhism which supplied the motive power for these attempts to wrest oneself from the bonds of a certain state of consciousness which was felt to be incomplete. As far as Western mysticism is concerned, its texts are full of instructions as to how man can and must release himself from the "I-ness" (*Ichhaftigkeit*) of his consciousness, so that through the knowledge of his being he may raise himself above it and reach the inward (godlike) man. Ruysbroeck makes use of an image which is also known to Indian philosophers, namely the tree that has its roots above and its top below,[1] "And he must climb up into the tree of belief, which grows downwards, since it has its roots in the godhead."[2] Ruysbroeck also says, like Yoga, "Man shall be free and without images, freed from all attachments and empty of all creatures."[3] "He must be untouched by lust and suffering, profit and loss, rising and falling, concern

[1] "There is the old tree, her roots grow upwards, her branches downwards.... It is called Brahman, and he alone is the undying." (*Katha-Upanishad*, II Adhyaya, 6 Valli, 1.)

It cannot be supposed that this Flemish mystic, who was born in 1273, borrowed this image from any Indian text.

[2] John of Ruysbroeck: *The Adornment of the Spiritual Marriage.* Transl. from the Flemish by C. A. Wynschek Dom, 1916, p. 47.

[3] Op. cit. p. 51.

about others, enjoyment and fear, and he shall not cling to any creature."[1] It is in this that the "unity" of the being consists, and this means "being turned inwards". This means "that a man is turned inwards, in his own heart, so that thereby he can feel and understand the inner working and the inner words of God".[2] This new condition of consciousness, arising from religious practice, is distinguished by the fact that outward things no longer affect an ego-like consciousness, whence a reciprocal attachment has arisen, but that an empty consciousness stands open to another influence. This "other" influence will no longer be felt as one's own activity, but as the work of a non-ego which has consciousness as its object.[3] It is as though the subject-character of the ego had been overrun, or taken over, by another subject which has taken the place of the ego.[4] It is a question of that well-known religious experience which has been formulated by St. Paul (*Gal.* ii, 20). Here a new condition of consciousness is undoubtedly described, separated from the former condition of consciousness by means of a far-reaching process of religious transformation.

It could be objected that *consciousness in itself* was not changed, but only the *consciousness of something*, just as though one had turned over the page of a book and now saw a different picture with the same eyes. I am afraid this conception is no more than an arbitrary interpretation, as it does not conform with the facts. The fact is that in the text it is not merely a different picture or object that is described, but rather the experience of a transformation, often resulting from the most violent convulsions. The erasing of one picture and its substitution by another is quite an everyday occurrence which has none of the attributes of a transformation experience. It is not that *something different is seen*, but that one *sees differently*. It is as though the spatial act of seeing were changed by a new dimension. When the master asks, "Do you hear the murmuring of the brook?" he obviously means something quite different from

[1] Op cit. p. 57.
[2] Op. cit. p. 62.
[3] "O Lord. . . . Instruct me in the doctrine of the non-ego," etc. (Quoted from Lankavatara-sutra. Suzuki: *Essays in Zen Buddhism*, I, p. 76.)
[4] A Zen master says, "Buddha is none other . . . who strives to see this mind." (Suzuki: *Essays in Zen Buddhism*, I, p. 76.)

ordinary "hearing".[1] Consciousness is something like perception, and just as the latter is subjected to conditions and limits, so is consciousness. For instance, one can be conscious at various stages, in a narrower or wider sphere, more superficially or more deeply. These differences of degree are, however, often differences of character, in that they depend completely upon the development of the personality—that is to say, upon the nature of the perceiving subject.

The intellect has no interest in the condition of the perceiving subject, in so far as the latter thinks only logically. The intellect is of necessity occupied with the digesting of the contents of the consciousness, and with the methods of digesting. It needs a philosophical passion to force the attempt to overcome the intellect and to push through to perception of the perceiving. Such a passion, however, is practically indistinguishable from religious motive power, and this whole problem belongs, therefore, to the religious transformation process, which is incommensurable with intellect. Antique philosophy is undoubtedly to a great extent at the service of the transformation process, which can be said less and less of the new philosophy. Schopenhauer is implicitly antique. Nietzsche's *Zarathustra* is, however, no philosophy but a dramatic transformation process, which has completely swallowed up intellect. It is no longer a question of thought, but in the highest sense of the thinker of thought—and this on every page of the book. A new man, a completely transformed man, is to appear on the scene, one who has broken the shell of the old man and who not only looks upon a new heaven and a new earth, but has created them. Angelus Silesius has expressed it rather more modestly than *Zarathustra*:

> *Mein Leib ist ein Schal, in dem ein Küchelein*
> *Vom Geist der Ewigkeit will ausgebrütet sein.*
> (My body is a shell, in which a chicken will be hatched
> from the spirit of eternity.)

Satori corresponds in the province of Christianity to a religious transformation experience. As there are, however, various

---

[1] Suzuk isays of this change, "The earlier form of contemplation is forsaken . . . the new beauty of the 'refreshing mind' or the 'glittering jewel'." (*Essays in Zen Buddhism*, I, p. 235.) See also p. 123.

degrees and types of such an experience, it would not be super-fluous to designate more exactly that category which corresponds most closely to the Zen experience. This is undoubtedly the mystic experience, distinguishable from similar experiences in that its preparation consists of "letting oneself go" (*sich lassen*), an "emptying of images" and other such things; this is in contrast to religious experiences which, like the Exercises of St. Ignatius, are based upon the practice and envisaging of holy images. I should like to include in this latter category transformation through belief and prayer, and through communal experience in Protestantism, since in this a very definite supposition plays the decisive role, and by no means "emptiness" or "release". The statement, characteristic of the latter state, "God is a Nothing", would be incompatible in principle with the contem-plation of passion, with belief and communal expectation.

Thus the analogy of *satori* with Western experience is confined to those few Christian mystics whose sayings for the sake of paradoxy skirt the border of heterodoxy or have actually over-stepped it. It was avowedly this quality that drew down upon Meister Eckehart the condemnation of the Church. If Buddhism were a "Church" in our sense of the word, the Zen movement would certainly have been an intolerable burden to her. The reason for this is the extremely individual form of the methods,[1] as also the iconoclastic attitude of many masters.[2] In so far as Zen is a movement, collective forms have been shaped in the course of the centuries, as can be seen from Suzuki's works on *The Training of the Zen Buddhist Monk*,[3] but in form and content they concern externals only. Apart from the type of habits, the way of spiritual training or forming seems to consist of *koan* methods. By *koan* is understood a paradoxical question, expression or action of the master. According to Suzuki's description it seems to be chiefly a matter of master questions

---

[1] "*Satori* is the most intimate of all individual experiences." (Suzuki: *Essays in Zen Buddhism*, I, p. 247.)

[2] A master says to his student, "I have actually nothing to tell you . . . and will never be your own." (Suzuki: *Essays in Zen Buddhism*, II, p. 69.)

A monk says to the master, "I have sought Buddha . . . upon which you are riding." (Suzuki: *Essays in Zen Buddhism*, II, p. 59.)

A master says: "Understanding which does not understand, that is Buddha. There is no other." (Suzuki: *Essays in Zen Buddhism*, II, p. 57.)

[3] Suzuki: *The Training of the Zen Buddhist Monk*. Kyoto, 1934.

handed down in the form of anecdotes. These are submitted by the teacher to the student for meditation. A classic example is the Wu- or Mu-anecdote. A monk once asked the master, "Has a dog Buddhist nature, too?", whereupon the master answered, "Wu." As Suzuki remarks, this "Wu" means quite simply "Wu", obviously just what the dog himself would have said in answer to the question.

At first glance it would appear that the submission of such a question as food for meditation would mean an anticipation or prejudicing of the final result, and that the contents of the meditation would be determined thereby, rather like the Jesuit Exercises, or certain Yogi meditations, the substance of which is determined by a task submitted by the teacher. The *koans*, however, are of such great variety, such ambiguity, and above all of such overwhelming paradoxy, that even an expert is completely in the dark as to what may emerge as a suitable solution. Moreover, the descriptions of the experiences are so obscure that in no single case could one perceive any unobjectionable rational connection between the *koan* and the experience. Since no logical succession can ever be proved, it is to be supposed that the *koan* method lays not the smallest restriction upon the freedom of the spiritual occurrences, and that the final result therefore comes from nothing but the *individual predisposition* of the initiate. The complete destruction of the rational intellect aimed at in the training creates an almost perfect lack of supposition of the consciousness. Conscious supposition is thereby excluded as far as possible, but not unconscious supposition; that is, the existing but unperceived psychological disposition, which is anything but emptiness and lack of supposition. It is a nature-given factor, and when it answers—as is obviously the *satori* experience—it is an answer of Nature, who has succeeded in conveying her reactions direct to the consciousness.[1] What the unconscious nature of the student opposes to the teacher or to the *koan* as an answer is manifestly *satori*. This, at least, appears to me to be the view which, by all descriptions, would express the essence of *satori* more or less correctly. This view is also supported by the fact

---

[1] Suzuki (*Essays in Zen Buddhism*, II, p. 46) says, ". . . Zen consciousness . . . which is a glimpse into the unconscious".

that the "glimpse into one's own nature", the "original man" and the depth of the being are often to the Zen master a matter of supreme concern.[1]

Zen differs from all other philosophic and religious meditation practices in its principle of *lack of supposition* (*Voraussetzung*). Buddha himself is sternly rejected; indeed, he is almost blasphemously ignored, although—or perhaps just because—he could be the strongest spiritual supposition of all. But he too is an image and must therefore be set aside. Nothing must be present except what is actually there; that is, man with his complete, unconscious supposition, of which, simply because it *is* unconscious, he can never, never rid himself. The answer which appears to come from a void, the light which flares up from the blackest darkness, these have always been experiences of wonderful and blessed illumination.

The world of consciousness is inevitably a world full of restrictions, of walls blocking the way. It is of necessity always one-sided, resulting from the essence of consciousness. No consciousness can harbour more than a very small number of simultaneous conceptions. All else must lie in shadow, withdrawn from sight. To increase the simultaneous content creates immediately a dimming of consciousness; confusion, in fact, to the point of disorientation. Consciousness does not simply demand, but *is*, of its very essence, a strict limitation to the few and hence the distinct. For our general orientation we are indebted simply and solely to the fact that through attentiveness we are able to effect a comparatively rapid succession of images. Attentiveness is, however, an effort of which we are not permanently capable. We have therefore to make do, so to speak, with a minimum of simultaneous perceptions and successions of images. Hence wide fields of possible perceptions are per-

---

[1] The 4th Maxim of Zen says, "Seeing into one's nature and the attainment of Buddhahood" (Suzuki: *Essays in Zen Buddhism*, I, p. 7). When a monk asked Hui-Neng for instruction he answered, "Show me your original face before you were born" (*Ibid.* 210). A Japanese Zen book says, "If you wish to seek the Buddha, see into your own Nature, for this Nature is the Buddha himself" (*Ibid.* p. 219). A *satori* experience reveals the "original man" to a Master (*Ibid.* 241). Hui-Neng said, "Think not of good, think not of evil, but see what at the moment thy own original features are, which thou hadst before coming into existence" (*Ibid.* 11, p. 28).

manently eliminated, and consciousness is always bound to the narrowest circle. What would happen if an individual consciousness were to succeed in embracing at one glance a simultaneous picture of all that it could imagine is beyond conception. If man has already succeeded in building up the structure of the world from the few clear things that he can perceive at one and the same time, what godly spectacle would present itself to his eyes were he able to perceive a great deal all at once and distinctly? This question only concerns perceptions that are *possible* to us. But if we add to those the unconscious contents —i.e. contents which are not yet, or no longer, capable of consciousness—and then try to imagine a complete spectacle, why, this is beyond the most audacious fantasy. This unimaginableness is of course a complete impossibility in the conscious form, but in the unconsciousness form it is a fact, inasmuch as all that is seething below is an ever-present potentiality of conception. The unconscious is an unglimpsable completeness of all subliminal psychic factors, a "total exhibition" of potential nature. It constitutes the entire disposition from which consciousness takes fragments from time to time. Now if consciousness is emptied as far as possible of its contents, the latter will fall into a state (at least a transitory state) of unconsciousness. This displacement ensues as a rule in Zen through the fact of the energy of the conscious being withdrawn from the contents and transferred either to the conception of emptiness or to the *koan*. As the two last-named must be stable, the succession of images is also abolished, and with it the energy which maintains the kinetic of the conscious. The amount of energy that is saved goes over to the unconscious, and reinforces its natural supply up to a certain maximum. This increases the readiness of the unconscious contents to break through to the conscious. Since the emptying and the closing down of the conscious is no easy matter, a special training and an indefinitely long period of time[1] is necessary to produce that maximum of tension which leads to the final break-through of unconscious contents into the conscious.

The contents which break through are by no means com-

---

[1] Bodhidharma, the Founder of Zen in China, says, ". . . Every effort of such men must miscarry." (Suzuki: *Essays in Zen Buddhism*, I, p. 176.)

pletely unspecified. As psychiatric experience with insanity shows, peculiar relations exist between the contents of the conscious and the delusions and deliria that break in upon it. They are the same relations as exist between the dreams and the working conscious of normal men. The connection is in substance a *compensatory*[1] *relationship*[2]: the contents of the unconscious bring to the surface everything necessary[3] in the broadest sense for the completion, i.e. *the completeness, of conscious orientation*. If the fragments offered by, or forced up from, the unconscious are successfully built into the life of the conscious, a psychic existence form results, which corresponds better to the whole of the individual personality, and therefore abolishes fruitless conflict between the conscious and the unconscious personality. Modern psycho-therapy rests upon this principle, inasmuch as it was able to break away from the historic prejudice that the unconscious harbours only infantile and morally inferior contents. There is certainly an inferior corner, a lumber-room of dirty secrets, which are however not so much unconscious as hidden and only half forgotten. But this has about as much to do with the whole of the unconscious as a hollow tooth has with the complete personality. The unconscious is the matrix of all metaphysical assertions, of all mythology, all philosophy (in so far as it is not merely critical) and all forms of life which are based upon psychological suppositions.

Every invasion of the unconscious is an answer to a definite condition of the conscious, and this answer follows from the whole of the idea-possibilities that are present; that is to say, from the complete disposition which, as explained above, is a simultaneous image *in potentia* of psychic existence. The splitting up into the single, the one-sided, the fragmentary character suits the essence of the conscious. The reaction from the disposition always has the character of completeness, as it corresponds with a nature which has not been divided up by any

[1] More probable than one that is purely complementary.
[2] For this I must refer the reader to medico-psychological specialist literature.
[3] This "necessity" is a working hypothesis. People can be, and are, of very different opinions about it. For instance, are religious conceptions "necessary"? Only the course of the individual life can decide this, i.e. individual experience. There are no abstract criteria for this.

discriminating conscious.[1] Hence its overpowering effect. It is the unexpected, comprehensive, completely illuminating answer, which operates all the more as illumination and revelation, since the conscious has wedged itself into a hopeless blind-alley.[2]

When therefore, after many years of the hardest practice and the most strenuous devastation of rational understanding, the Zen student receives an answer—the only true answer—from Nature herself, everything that is said of *satori* can be understood. As can easily be seen, it is the *naturelike-ness* (*Naturhaftigkeit*) of the answer which shines forth from most of the Zen anecdotes. Yes, one can accept with complete complaisance the enlightened student who, as one story relates, wished his master a sound thrashing as a reward (see pages 93–4). How much wisdom lies in the master's "Wu", the answer to the question about the Buddha nature of the dog! One must always consider, however, that on the one hand there are any number of people who cannot distinguish between a spiritual witticism and nonsense, and on the other hand very many people who are convinced of their own cleverness to such an extent that they have never in their lives met any but fools.

Great as is the value of Zen Buddhism for the understanding of the religious transformation process, its use among Western people is very improbable. The spiritual conceptions necessary to Zen are missing in the West. Who amongst us would produce such implicit trust in a superior master and his incomprehensible ways? This respect for the greater human personality exists only in the East. Who could boast of believing in the possibility of a transformation experience paradoxical beyond measure; to the extent, moreover, of sacrificing many years of his life to the wearisome pursuit of such an object? And finally, who would dare to take upon himself the authority of a heterodoxical transformation experience? Let it be a man of little trustworthiness, one who, maybe from pathological reasons, has too much to say for himself; such a man would have no cause to

[1] "When mind discriminates, there is manifoldness of things; when it does not it looks into the true state of things." (Suzuki: *Essays in Zen Buddhism*, I, p. 88.)

[2] See the passage beginning, "Have your mind like unto space. . . ." (Suzuki: *Essays in Zen Buddhism*, I, p. 209.)

complain of any lack of following among us. But if the "Master" sets a hard task, which requires more than a lot of parrot talk, the European begins to have doubts, for the steep path of self-development is to him as mournful and dark as Hell.

I have no doubt that the *satori* experience does occur also in the West, for we too have men who scent ultimate ends and will spare themselves no pains to draw near to them. But they will keep silence, not only out of shyness but because they know that any attempt to convey their experiences to others would be hopeless. For there is nothing in our culture approaching these aspirations, not even the Church, the custodian of religious goods. It is in fact her function to oppose all such extreme experiences, for these can only be heterodox. The only movement within our culture which partly has, and partly should have, some understanding of these aspirations is psychotherapy. It is therefore not a matter of chance that this foreword is written by a psychotherapist.

Taken basically, psychotherapy is a dialectic relationship between the doctor and the patient. It is a discussion between two spiritual wholes, in which all wisdom is merely a tool. The goal is transformation; not indeed a predetermined, but rather an indeterminable, change, the only criterion of which is the disappearance of I-ness. No efforts on the part of the doctor force the experience. The most he can do is to make easy the path of the patient towards the attainment of an attitude which will oppose the least resistance to the decisive experience. If knowledge plays no small part in our Western procedure, this is equivalent to the importance of the traditional spiritual atmosphere of Buddhism in Zen. Zen and its technique could only exist on the basis of Buddhist spiritual culture, and this is its premise. You cannot destroy a rationalist intellect that was never present. A Zen adept is not the outcome of ignorance and lack of culture. Hence even with us it happens not infrequently that a conscious ego and a conscious, cultivated understanding must first be produced by therapy before one can even think about abolishing I-ness or rationalism. Moreover, psychotherapy is by no means dealing with men who, like Zen monks, are ready to make any sacrifice for the sake of truth, but very often with the most stubborn of all Europeans. Thus the tasks of psychotherapy are of course much more varied, and the individual phases of the long process meet with far more opposition than in Zen.

For these and many other reasons a direct transmission of Zen to Western conditions is neither commendable nor even possible. The psychotherapist, however, who is seriously concerned with the question of the aims of his therapy cannot be unmoved when he sees what ultimate result an oriental method of spiritual "healing"—i.e. "making whole"—is striving for. It is a well-known fact that this problem has been seriously occupying the most venturesome minds of the East for more than two thousand years, and that in this respect methods and philosophical doctrines have been developed which simply put all Western attempts in the same line into the shade. Our attempts—with a few exceptions—have all stopped short at either magic (mystery cults, among which Christianity must be counted) or the intellectual (philosophers from Pythagoras to Schopenhauer). It is only the spiritual tragedies of Goethe's *Faust* and Nietzsche's *Zarathustra* which mark the first glimmerings of the break-through of a total experience (*Ganzheitserlebnis*) in our Western hemisphere.[1] And we do not even know today what these, the most promising of all products of the European mind, may at length signify, so overlaid are they with all the materiality and obviousness of our preformed Greek spirit.[2] Although our intellect has brought well-nigh to perfection the ability of the bird of prey to espy the tiniest mouse from the greatest height, the gravity of earth seizes him and the Sangskaras entangle him in a world of confusing pictures if he no longer looks for booty but turns at least one eye inwards *to find him who seeks*. Yes, he falls into the travail of a demoniacal birth, beset with unknown terrors and dangers and menaced by deluding mirages and labyrinthine mazes. The worst of all fates threatens the venturer; the silent, abysmal *loneliness* in the time which he calls his own. Who knows anything

[1] In this connection I must mention also the English mystic, William Blake. Cf. the excellent representation in Milton O. Percival's *William Blake's Circle of Destiny*. Columbia University Press, 1938.

[2] The genius of the Greek signifies the break-through of the conscious into the materiality of the world, whereby the latter was robbed of her original dreamlikeness.

about the deep motives for the "masterpiece", as Goethe called *Faust*, or the shudders of the "Dionysus Experience"? One must read *Bardo Thödol*, the Tibetan Book of the Dead, backwards, as I have suggested,[1] in order to find an Eastern parallel to the torments and catastrophes of the Western "way of release" to completeness. This is what matters—not good intentions, clever imitations or even intellectual acrobatics. Such, in intimations or in greater or lesser fragments, appears before the psychotherapist who has freed himself from rash and short-sighted doctrinal opinions. If he is a slave to his quasi-biological creed he will always try to reduce what he observes to the banal familiar, and to bring it thereby to a rationalistic denominator which only suffices one who is content with illusions. The foremost of all illusions, however, is that something can suffice someone. That illusion stands behind all that is unendurable and in front of all progress, and it is one of the most difficult things to overcome. If the psychotherapist finds time from his helpful activities for a little reflection, or if by any chance he is forced into seeing through his own illusions, it may dawn upon him how hollow and flat, indeed how contrary to life are all rationalistic reductions when they come upon something alive, that will develop. If he follows this up he soon gets an idea of what it means "to tear open those doors which everyone would gladly slink past".

I would not under any circumstances have it understood that in what I have said above I am making any recommendation or offering any advice. But when Western men begin to talk about Zen I consider it my duty to show the European where our entrance lies to that "longest of all roads" which leads to *satori*, and what difficulties strew that path, which has been trodden by only a few of our great men—perhaps as a beacon on a high mountain, shining out in the hazy future. It would be an unhealthy mistake to assume that *satori* or *samadhi* are to be met with anywhere below those heights. For a complete experience there can be nothing cheaper or smaller than the whole. The psychological significance of this can be understood by the simple consideration of the fact that the conscious is only a part of the spiritual, and is never therefore capable of spiritual

[1] W. Y. Evans-Wentz: *Das Tibetanische Totenbuch*. Rascher, Zurich, 1934.

completeness: for that the indefinite expansion of the unconscious is needed. The latter, however, can neither be captured
with skilful formulae nor exorcized by means of scientific dogmas,
for there is something of Destiny clinging to it—yes, it is sometimes Destiny itself, as *Faust* and *Zarathustra* show all too clearly.
The attainment of completeness calls for the use of the whole.
Nothing less will do; hence there can be no easier conditions,
no substitution, no compromise. Inasmuch as both *Faust* and
Zarathustra, despite the highest appreciation, are only on the
border-line of what is comprehensible to the European, one can
scarcely expect a cultured public who have only just begun
to hear about the dim world of the soul to be able to form any
adequate conception of the spiritual state of a man who has
fallen into the confusions of the *individuation process*, by which
term I have designated the "becoming whole" (*Ganzwerdung*).
People drag forth the vocabulary of pathology, they console
themselves with "neurosis" and "psychosis" terminology,
whisper about "creative mystery"—but what can a man who
is probably not a poet create? The last-mentioned misunderstanding has in modern times caused not a few people to call
themselves of their own grace "artists". As if "art" had nothing
at all to do with "ability"! If you have nothing to "create",
perhaps you create yourself.

Zen shows how much "becoming whole" means to the East.
Preoccupation with the riddles of Zen may perhaps stiffen the
spine of the faint-hearted European, or provide a pair of spec-
tacles for his shortsightedness, so that from his "gloomy hole
in the wall" he may enjoy at least a glimpse of the world of
spiritual experience, which until now has been shrouded in
mist. It will certainly not end badly, for those who are terrified
will be effectively protected from further corruption, as also
from everything of significance, by the helpful idea of "auto-
suggestion" (see page 93). I should like to warn the attentive
and sympathetic reader, however, not to underestimate the
spiritual depth of the East, or to assume any kind of cheapness
in Zen.[1] The zealously nurtured attitude of literal credulity

---

[1] "Zen is not a pastime, but the most serious task in life. No empty head
will ever venture near it." (Suzuki: *Essays in Zen Buddhism*, I, p. 16.) See also
p. 78.

towards the oriental treasure of thought is in this case a lesser danger, as in Zen there are fortunately none of those marvellously incomprehensible words, as in Indian cults. Neither does Zen play about with complicated Hatha-yoga techniques,[1] which delude the physiologically thinking European with the false hope that the spirit can be obtained by sitting and by breathing. On the contrary, Zen demands intelligence and will-power, as do all the greater things which desire to become real.

---

[1] "When you seek Buddhahood . . . you will never attain the truth," says a master. (Suzuki: *Essays in Zen Buddhism*, I, p. 222.)

.

I

PRELIMINARY

Buddhism in its course of development has completed a form which distinguishes itself from its so-called primitive or original type—so greatly, indeed, that we are justified in emphasizing its historical division into two schools, Hinayana and Mahayana, or the Lesser Vehicle and the Greater Vehicle of salvation. As a matter of fact, the Mahayana, with all its varied formulae, is no more than a developed form of Buddhism and traces back its final authority to its Indian founder, the great Buddha Sakyamuni. When this developed form of the Mahayana was introduced into China and then into Japan, it achieved further development in these countries. This achievement was no doubt due to the Chinese and Japanese Buddhist leaders, who knew how to apply the principles of their faith to the ever-varying conditions of life and to the religious needs of the people. And this elaboration and adaptation on their part has still further widened the gap that has already been in existence between the Mahayana[1] and its more primitive type. At present the Mahayana form may be said not to display, superficially at least, those features most conspicuously characteristic of original Buddhism.

[1] To be accurate, the fundamental ideas of the Mahayana are expounded in the Prajnaparamita group of Buddhist literature, the earliest of which must have appeared at the latest within three hundred years of the Buddha's death. The germs are no doubt in the writings belonging to the so-called primitive Buddhism. Only their development, that is, a conscious grasp of them as most essential in the teachings of the founder, could not be effected without his followers' actually living the teachings for some time through the variously changing conditions of life. Thus enriched in experience and matured in reflection, the Indian Buddhists came to have the Mahayana form of Buddhism as distinguished from its primitive or original form. In India two Mahayana schools are known: the Madhyamika of Nagarjuna and the Vijnaptimatra or Yogacara of Asanga and Vasubandhu. In China more schools developed: the Tendai (*t'ien-tai*), the Kegon (*avatamsaka*), the Jodo (*ching-t'u*), the Zen (*ch'an*), etc. In Japan we have besides these the Hokke, the Shingon, the Shin, the Ji, etc. All these schools or sects belong to the Mahayana wing of Buddhism.

For this reason there are people who would declare that this branch of Buddhism is in reality no Buddhism in the sense that the latter is commonly understood. My contention, however, is this: anything that has life in it is an organism, and it is in the very nature of an organism that it never remains in the same state of existence. An acorn is quite different, even as a young oak with tender leaves just out of its protective shell is quite different from a full-grown tree so stately and gigantic and towering up to the sky. But throughout these varying phases of change there is a continuation of growth and unmistakable marks of identity, whence we know that one and the same plant has passed through many stages of becoming. The so-called primitive Buddhism is the seed; out of it Far-Eastern Buddhism has come into existence with the promise of still further growth. Scholars may talk of historical Buddhism, but my subject here is to see Buddhism not only in its historical development but from the point of view of its still vitally concerning us as a quickening spiritual force in the Far East.

Among the many sects of Buddhism that have grown up, especially in China and Japan, we find a unique order claiming to transmit the essence and spirit of Buddhism directly from its author, and this not through any secret document or by means of any mysterious rite. This order is one of the most significant aspects of Buddhism, not only from the point of view of its historical importance and spiritual vitality, but from the point of view of its most original and stimulating manner of demonstration. The "Doctrine of the Buddha-heart (*buddhahridaya*)" is its scholastic name, but more commonly it is known as "Zen". That Zen is not the same as Dhyana, though the term *Zen* is derived from the Chinese transliteration (*ch'an-na*; *zenna* in Japanese) of the original Sanskrit, will be explained later on.

This school is unique in various ways in the history of religion. Its doctrines, theoretically stated, may be said to be those of speculative mysticism, but they are presented and demonstrated in such a manner that only those initiates who, after long training, have actually gained an insight into the system can understand their ultimate signification. To those who have not acquired this penetrating knowledge, that is, to those who have not experienced Zen in their everyday active life—its teachings, or rather its utterances, assume quite a peculiar, uncouth, and even enigmatical aspect. Such people, looking at Zen more or less conceptually, consider Zen utterly absurd and ludicrous, or deliberately making itself unintelligible in order to guard its apparent profundity against outside criticism. But, according to the followers of Zen, its apparently paradoxical statements are not artificialities contrived to hide themselves behind a screen of obscurity; but simply because the human tongue is not an adequate organ for expressing the deepest truths of Zen, the latter cannot be made the subject of logical exposition; they are to be experienced in the inmost soul when they become for the first time intelligible. In point of fact, no plainer and more straightforward expressions than those of Zen have ever been made by any other branch of human experience. "Coal is black"—this is plain enough; but Zen protests, "Coal is not black." This is also plain enough, and indeed even plainer than the first positive statement when we come right down to the truth of the matter.

Personal experience, therefore, is everything in Zen. No ideas are intelligible to those who have no backing of experience. This is a platitude. A baby has no ideas, for its mentality is not yet so developed as to experience anything in the way of ideas. If it has them at all, they must be something extremely obscure and blurred and not in correspondence with realities. To get the clearest and most efficient understanding of a thing, therefore, it must be experienced personally. Especially when the thing is concerned with life itself, personal experience is an absolute necessity. Without this experience nothing relative to its profound working will ever be accurately and therefore efficiently grasped. The foundation of all concepts is simple, unsophisticated experience. Zen places the utmost emphasis upon this foundation-experience, and it is around this that Zen constructs all the verbal and conceptual scaffold which is found in its literature known as "Sayings" (goroku, J.; yu-lu, Ch.). Though the scaffold affords a most useful means to reach the inmost reality, it is still an elaboration and artificiality. We lose its whole significance when it is taken for a final reality. The nature of the human understanding compels us not to put too much confidence in the superstructure. Mystification is far from being the object

33

of Zen itself, but to those who have not touched the central fact of life Zen inevitably appears as mystifying. Penetrate through the conceptual superstructure and what is imagined to be a mystification will at once disappear, and at the same time there will be an enlightenment known as *satori*.[1]

Zen, therefore, most strongly and persistently insists on an inner spiritual experience. It does not attach any intrinsic importance to the sacred sutras or to their exegeses by the wise and learned. Personal experience is strongly set against authority and objective revelation, and as the most practical method of attaining spiritual enlightenment the followers of Zen propose the practice of Dhyana, known as *zazen*[2] in Japanese.

A few words must be said here in regard to the systematic training by Zen of its followers in the attainment of the spiritual insight which has been referred to before as the foundation-experience of Zen. For this is where Zen pre-eminently distinguishes itself from other forms of mysticism. To most mystics such spiritual experience, so intensely personal, comes as something sporadic, isolated, and unexpected. Christians use prayer, or mortification, or contemplation so called, as the means of bringing this on themselves, and leave its fulfilment to divine grace. But as Buddhism does not recognize a supernatural agency in such matters, the Zen method of spiritual training is practical and systematic. From the beginning of its history in China there has been such a tendency well marked; but, as time went on, a regular system has finally come into existence, and the Zen school at present has a thoroughgoing method for its followers to train themselves in the attainment of their object. Herein lies the practical merit of Zen. While it is highly speculative on the one hand, its methodical discipline on the other hand produces most fruitful and beneficial results on moral character. We sometimes forget its highly abstract character when it is expressed in connection with the facts of our everyday practical life; but here it is where we have to appreciate the real value of Zen, for Zen finds an inexpressibly deep thought even

---

[1] See below.

[2] *Za* means "to sit", and *zazen* may be summarily taken as meaning "to sit in meditation". What it exactly signifies will be seen later in connection with the description of "The Meditation Hall" (*zendo*, J.; *ch'an-t'ang*, Ch.).

in holding up a finger, or in saying a "good morning" to a friend casually met on the street. In the eye of Zen the most practical is the most abstruse, and *vice versa*. All the system of discipline adopted by Zen is the outcome of this fundamental experience.

I said that Zen is mystical. This is inevitable, seeing that Zen is the keynote of Oriental culture; it is what makes the West frequently fail to fathom exactly the depths of the Oriental mind, for mysticism in its very nature defies the analysis of logic, and logic is the most characteristic feature of Western thought. The East is synthetic in its method of reasoning; it does not care so much for the elaboration of particulars as for a comprehensive grasp of the whole, and this intuitively. Therefore the Eastern mind, if we assume its existence, is necessarily vague and indefinite, and seems not to have an index which at once reveals the contents to an outsider. The thing is there before our eyes, for it refuses to be ignored; but when we endeavour to grasp it in our own hands in order to examine it more closely or systematically, it eludes and we lose its track. Zen is provokingly evasive. This is not due of course to any conscious or premeditated artifice with which the Eastern mind schemes to shun the scrutiny of others. The unfathomableness is in the very constitution, so to speak, of the Eastern mind. Therefore, to understand the East we must understand mysticism; that is, Zen.

It is to be remembered, however, that there are various types of mysticism, rational and irrational, speculative and occult, sensible and fantastic. When I say that the East is mystical, I do not mean that the East is fantastic, irrational, and altogether impossible to bring within the sphere of intellectual comprehension. What I mean is simply that in the working of the Eastern mind there is something calm, quiet, silent, undisturbable, which appears as if always looking into eternity. This quietude and silence, however, does not point to mere idleness or inactivity. The silence is not that of the desert shorn of all vegetation, nor is it that of a corpse forever gone to sleep and decay. It is the silence of an "eternal abyss" in which all contrasts and conditions are buried; it is the silence of God who, deeply absorbed in contemplation of his works past, present, and future, sits

35

calmly on his throne of absolute oneness and allness. It is the "silence of thunder" obtained in the midst of the flash and uproar of opposing electric currents. This sort of silence pervades all things Oriental. Woe unto those who take it for decadence and death, for they will be overwhelmed by an overwhelming outburst of activity out of the eternal silence. It is in this sense that I speak of the mysticism of Oriental culture. And I can affirm that the cultivation of this kind of mysticism is principally due to the influence of Zen. If Buddhism were to develop in the Far East so as to satisfy the spiritual cravings of its people, it had to grow into Zen. The Indians are mystical, but their mysticism is too speculative, too contemplative, too complicated, and, moreover, it does not seem to have any real, vital relation with the practical world of particulars in which we are living. The Far-Eastern mysticism, on the contrary, is direct, practical, and surprisingly simple. This could not develop into anything else but Zen.

All the other Buddhist sects in China as well as in Japan bespeak their Indian origin in an unmistakable manner. For their metaphysical complexity, their long-winded phraseology, their highly abstract reasoning, their penetrating insight into the nature of things, and their comprehensive interpretation of affairs relating to life, are most obviously Indian and not at all Chinese or Japanese. This will be recognized at once by all those who are acquainted with Far-Eastern Buddhism. For instance, look at those extremely complex rites as practised by the Shingon sect, and also at their elaborate systems of "Mandala", by means of which they try to explain the universe. No Chinese or Japanese mind would have conceived such an intricate net-work of philosophy without being first influenced by Indian thought. Then observe how highly speculative is the philosophy of the Madhyamika, the Tendai (*T'ien-tai* in C.), or Kegon (*Avatamsaka* or *Gandavyuha* in Sanskrit). Their abstraction and logical acumen are truly amazing. These facts plainly show that those sects of Far-Eastern Buddhism are at bottom foreign importations.

But when we come to Zen, after a survey of the general field of Buddhism, we are compelled to acknowledge that its simplicity, its directness, its pragmatic tendency, and its close connection with everyday life stand in remarkable contrast to the other Buddhist sects. Undoubtedly the main ideas of Zen are derived from Buddhism, and we cannot but consider it a legitimate development of the latter; but this development has been achieved in order to meet the requirements peculiarly characteristic of the psychology of the Far-Eastern people. The spirit of Buddhism has left its highly metaphysical super-structure in order to become a practical discipline of life. The result is Zen. Therefore I make bold to say that in Zen are found systematized, or rather crystallized, all the philosophy, religion, and life itself of the Far-Eastern people, especially of the Japanese.

II

WHAT IS ZEN?

Before proceeding to expound the teaching of Zen at some length in the following pages, let me answer some of the questions which are frequently raised by critics concerning the real nature of Zen.

Is Zen a system of philosophy, highly intellectual and profoundly metaphysical, as most Buddhist teachings are?

I have already stated that we find in Zen all the philosophy of the East crystallized, but this ought not to be taken as meaning that Zen is a philosophy in the ordinary application of the term. Zen is decidedly not a system founded upon logic and analysis. If anything, it is the antipode to logic, by which I mean the dualistic mode of thinking. There may be an intellectual element in Zen, for Zen is the whole mind, and in it we find a great many things; but the mind is not a composite thing that is to be divided into so many faculties, leaving nothing behind when the dissection is over. Zen has nothing to teach us in the way of intellectual analysis; nor has it any set doctrines which are imposed on its followers for acceptance. In this respect Zen is quite chaotic if you choose to say so. Probably Zen followers may have sets of doctrines, but they have them on their own account, and for their own benefit; they do not owe the fact to Zen. Thereore, there are in Zen no sacred books or dogmatic tenets, nor are there any symbolic formulae through which an access might be gained into the signification of Zen. If I am asked, then, what Zen teaches, I would answer, Zen teaches nothing. Whatever teachings there are in Zen, they come out of one's own mind. We teach ourselves; Zen merely points the way. Unless this pointing is teaching, there is certainly nothing in Zen purposely set up as its cardinal doctrines or as its fundamental philosophy.

Zen claims to be Buddhism, but all the Buddhist teachings as propounded in the sutras and sastras are treated by Zen as mere waste paper whose utility consists in wiping off the dirt of

38

intellect and nothing more. Do not imagine, however, that Zen is nihilism. All nihilism is self-destructive, it ends nowhere. Negativism is sound as method, but the highest truth is an affirmation. When it is said that Zen has no philosophy, that it denies all doctrinal authority, that it casts aside all so-called sacred literature as rubbish, we must not forget that Zen is holding up in this very act of negation something quite positive and eternally affirmative. This will become clearer as we proceed.

Is Zen a religion? It is not a religion in the sense that the term is popularly understood; for Zen has no God to worship, no ceremonial rites to observe, no future abode to which the dead are destined, and, last of all, Zen has no soul whose welfare is to be looked after by somebody else and whose immortality is a matter of intense concern with some people. Zen is free from all these dogmatic and "religious" encumbrances.

When I say there is no God in Zen, the pious reader may be shocked, but this does not mean that Zen denies the existence of God; neither denial nor affirmation concerns Zen. When a thing is denied, the very denial involves something not denied. The same can be said of affirmation. This is inevitable in logic. Zen wants to rise above logic, Zen wants to find a higher affirmation where there are no antitheses. Therefore, in Zen, God is neither denied nor insisted upon; only there is in Zen no such God as has been conceived by Jewish and Christian minds. For the same reason that Zen is not a philosophy, Zen is not a religion.

As to all those images of various Buddhas and Bodhisattvas and Devas and other beings that one comes across in Zen temples, they are like so many pieces of wood or stone or metal; they are like the camellias, azalias, or stone lanterns in my garden. Make obeisance to the camellia now in full bloom, and worship it if you like, Zen would say. There is as much religion in so doing as in bowing to the various Buddhist gods, or as sprinkling holy water, or as participating in the Lord's Supper. All those pious deeds considered to be meritorious or sanctifying by most so-called religiously minded people are artificialities in the eyes of Zen. It boldly declares that "the immaculate Yogins do not enter Nirvana and the precept-violating monks do not gc to hell". This, to ordinary minds, is a contradiction of the common law of moral life, but herein lies the truth and life of Zen. Zen is the spirit of a man. Zen believes in his inner purity and goodness. Whatever is superadded or violently torn away, injures the wholesomeness of the spirit. Zen, therefore, is emphatically against all religious conventionalism.

Its irreligion, however, is merely apparent. Those who are truly religious will be surprised to find that after all there is so much of religion in the barbarous declaration of Zen. But to say that Zen is a religion, in the sense that Christianity or Mohammedanism is, would be a mistake. To make my point clearer, I quote the following. When Sakyamuni was born, it is said that he lifted one hand toward the heavens and pointed to the earth with the other, exclaiming, "Above the heavens and below the heavens, I alone am the Honoured One!" Ummon (Yun-men), founder of the Ummon School of Zen, comments on this by saying, "If I had been with him at the moment of his uttering this, I would surely have struck him dead with one blow and thrown the corpse into the maw of a hungry dog." What unbelievers would ever think of making such raving remarks over a spiritual leader? Yet one of the Zen masters following Ummon says: "Indeed, this is the way Ummon desires to serve the world, sacrificing everything he has, body and mind! How grateful he must have felt for the love of Buddha!"

Zen is not to be confounded with a form of meditation as practised by "New Thought" people, or Christian Scientists, or Hindu Sannyasins, or some Buddhists. Dhyana, as it is understood by Zen, does not correspond to the practice as carried on in Zen. A man may meditate on a religious or philosophical subject while disciplining himself in Zen, but that is only incidental; the essence of Zen is not there at all. Zen purposes to discipline the mind itself, to make it its own master, through an insight into its proper nature. This getting into the real nature of one's own mind or soul is the fundamental object of Zen Buddhism. Zen, therefore, is more than meditation and Dhyana in its ordinary sense. The discipline of Zen consists in opening the mental eye in order to look into the very reason of existence.

To meditate, a man has to fix his thought on something; for instance, on the oneness of God, or his infinite love, or on the impermanence of things. But this is the very thing Zen desires to avoid. If there is anything Zen strongly emphasizes it is the attainment of freedom; that is, freedom from all unnatural encumbrances. Meditation is something artificially put on; it does not belong to the native activity of the mind. Upon what do the fowl of the air meditate? Upon what do the fish in the water meditate? They fly; they swim. Is not that enough? Who wants to fix his mind on the unity of God and man, or on the nothingness of this life? Who wants to be arrested in the daily manifestations of his life-activity by such meditations as the goodness of a divine being or the everlasting fire of hell?

We may say that Christianity is monotheistic, and the Vedanta pantheistic; but we cannot make a similar assertion about Zen. Zen is neither monotheistic nor pantheistic; Zen defies all such designations. Hence there is no object in Zen upon which to fix the thought. Zen is a wafting cloud in the sky. No screw fastens it, no string holds it; it moves as it lists. *No amount of meditation will keep Zen in one place.* Meditation is not Zen. Neither pantheism nor monotheism provides Zen with its subjects of concentration. If Zen is monotheistic, it may tell its followers to meditate on the oneness of things where all differences and inequalities, enveloped in the all-illuminating brightness of the divine light, are obliterated. If Zen were pantheistic it would tell us that every meanest flower in the field reflects the glory of God. But what Zen says is "After all things are reduced to oneness, where would that One be reduced?" Zen wants to have one's mind free and unobstructed; even the idea of oneness or allness is a stumbling-block and a strangling snare which threatens the original freedom of the spirit.

Zen, therefore, does not ask us to concentrate our thought on the idea that a dog is God, or that three pounds of flax are divine. When Zen does this it commits itself to a definite system of philosophy, and there is no more Zen. Zen just feels fire warm and ice cold, because when it freezes we shiver and welcome fire. The feeling is all in all, as Faust declares; all our theorization fails to touch reality. But "the feeling" here must be understood in its deepest sense or in its purest form. Even to say that "This is the

41

feeling" means that Zen is no more there. Zen defies all concept-making. That is why Zen is difficult to grasp.

Whatever meditation Zen may propose, then, will be to take things as they are, to consider snow white and the raven black. When we speak of meditation we in most cases refer to its abstract character; that is, meditation is known to be the con-centration of the mind on some highly generalized proposition, which is, in the nature of things, not always closely and directly connected with the concrete affairs of life. Zen perceives or feels, and does not abstract nor meditate. Zen penetrates and is finally lost in the immersion. Meditation, on the other hand, is out-spokenly dualistic and consequently inevitably superficial.

One critic[1] regards Zen as "the Buddhist counterpart of the 'Spiritual Exercises' of St. Ignatius Loyala". The critic shows a great inclination to find Christian analogies for things Budd-histic, and this is one of such instances. Those who have at all a clear understanding of Zen will at once see how wide of the mark this comparison is. Even superficially speaking, there is not a shadow of similitude between the exercises of Zen and those proposed by the founder of the Society of Jesus. The contem-plations and prayers of St. Ignatius are, from the Zen point of view, merely so many fabrications of the imagination elaborately woven for the benefit of the piously minded; and in reality this is like piling tiles upon tiles on one's head, and there is no true gain in the life of the spirit. We can say this, however, that those "Spiritual Exercises" in some ways resemble certain medi-tations of Hinayana Buddhism, such as the Five Mind-quieting Methods, or the Nine Thoughts on Impurity, or the Six or Ten Subjects of Memory.

Zen is sometimes made to mean "mind-murder and the curse of idle reverie". This is the statement of Griffis, the well-known author of *Religions of Japan*.[2] By "mind-murder" I do not know what he really means, but does he mean that Zen kills the activities of the mind by making one's thought fix on one thing, or by inducing sleep? Mr. Reischauer in his book[3] almost endorses this view of Griffis by asserting that Zen is "mystical self-intoxi-cation". Does he mean that Zen is intoxicated in the "Greater

[1] Arthur Lloyd: *Wheat Among the Tares*, p. 53.   [2] P. 255.
[3] *Studies of Buddhism in Japan*, p. 118.

Self"; so called, as Spinoza was intoxicated in God? Though Mr. Reischauer is not quite clear as to the meaning of "intoxication", he may think that Zen is unduly absorbed in the thought of the "Greater Self" as the final reality in this world of particulars. It is amazing to see how superficial some of the uncritical observers of Zen are! In point of fact, Zen has no "mind" to murder; therefore, there is no "mind-murdering" in Zen. Zen has again no "self" as something to which we can cling as a refuge; therefore, in Zen again there is no "self" by which we may become intoxicated.

The truth is, Zen is extremely elusive as far as its outward aspects are concerned; when you think you have caught a glimpse of it, it is no more there; from afar it looks so approachable, but as soon as you come near it you see it even further away from you than before. Unless, therefore, you devote some years of earnest study to the understanding of its primary principles, it is not to be expected that you will begin to have a fair grasp of Zen.

"The way to ascend unto God is to descend into one's self";— these are Hugo's words. "If thou wishest to search out the deep things of God, search out the depths of thine own spirit";—this comes from Richard of St. Victor. When all these deep things are searched out there is after all no "self". Where you can descend, there is no "spirit", no "God" whose depths are to be fathomed. Why? Because Zen is a bottomless abyss. Zen declares, though in a somewhat different manner: "Nothing really exists throughout the triple world; where do you wish to see the mind (or spirit = *hsin*)? The four elements are all empty in their ultimate nature; where could the Buddha's abode be?—but lo! the truth is unfolding itself right before your eye. This is all there is to it—and indeed nothing more!" A minute's hesitation and Zen is irrevocably lost. All the Buddhas of the past, present, and future may try to make you catch it once more, and yet it is a thousand miles away. "Mind-murder" and "self-intoxication", forsooth! Zen has no time to bother itself with such criticisms.

The critics may mean that the mind is hypnotized by Zen to a state of unconsciousness, and that when this obtains, the favourite Buddhist doctrine of emptiness (*sunyata*) is realized, where the subject is not conscious of an objective world or of

43

himself, being lost in one vast emptiness, whatever this may be. This interpretation again fails to hit Zen aright. It is true that there are some such expressions in Zen as might suggest this kind of interpretation, but to understand Zen we must make a leap here. The "vast emptiness" must be traversed. The subject must be awakened from a state of unconsciousness if he does not wish to be buried alive. Zen is attained only when "self-intoxication" is abandoned and the "drunkard" is really awakened to his deeper self. If the mind is ever to be "murdered", leave the work in the hand of Zen; for it is Zen that will restore the murdered and lifeless one into a state of eternal life. "Be born again, be awakened from the dream, rise from the death, O ye drunkards!" Zen would exclaim. Do not try, therefore, to see Zen with the eyes bandaged; and your hands are too unsteady to take hold of it. And remember I am not indulging in figures of speech.

I might multiply many such criticisms if it were necessary but I hope that the above have sufficiently prepared the reader's mind for the following more positive statements concerning Zen. The basic idea of Zen is to come in touch with the inner workings of our being, and to do this in the most direct way possible, without resorting to anything external or superadded. Therefore, anything that has the semblance of an external authority is rejected by Zen. Absolute faith is placed in a man's own inner being. For whatever authority there is in Zen, all comes from within. This is true in the strictest sense of the word. Even the reasoning faculty is not considered final or absolute. On the contrary, it hinders the mind from coming into the directest communication with itself. The intellect accomplishes its mission when it works as an intermediary, and Zen has nothing to do with an intermediary except when it desires to communicate itself to others. For this reason all the scriptures are merely tentative and provisory; there is in them no finality. The central fact of life as it is lived is what Zen aims to grasp, and this in the most direct and most vital manner. Zen professes itself to be the spirit of Buddhism, but in fact it is the spirit of all religions and philosophies. When Zen is thoroughly understood, absolute peace of mind is attained, and a man lives as he ought to live. What more may we hope?

Some say that as Zen is admittedly a form of mysticism it

44

cannot claim to be unique in the history of religion. Perhaps so; but Zen is a mysticism of its own order. It is mystical in the sense that the sun shines, that the flower blooms, that I hear at this moment somebody beating a drum in the street. If these are mystical facts, Zen is brim-full of them. When a Zen master was once asked what Zen was, he replied, "Your everyday thought." Is this not plain and most straightforward? It has nothing to do with any sectarian spirit. Christians as well as Buddhists can practise Zen just as big fish and small fish are both contentedly living in the same ocean. Zen is the ocean, Zen is the air, Zen is the mountain, Zen is thunder and lightning, the spring flower, summer heat, and winter snow; nay, more than that, Zen is the man. With all the formalities, conventionalisms, and superadditions that Zen has accumulated in its long history, its central fact is very much alive. The special merit of Zen lies in this: that we are still able to see into this ultimate fact without being biased by anything.

As has been said before, what makes Zen unique as it is practised in Japan is its systematic training of the mind. Ordinary mysticism has been too erratic a product and apart from one's ordinary life; this Zen has revolutionized. What was up in the heavens, Zen has brought down to earth. With the development of Zen, mysticism has ceased to be mystical; it is no more the spasmodic product of an abnormally endowed mind. For Zen reveals itself in the most uninteresting and uneventful life of a plain man of the street, recognizing the fact of living in the midst of life as it is lived. Zen systematically trains the mind to see this; it opens a man's eye to the greatest mystery as it is daily and hourly performed; it enlarges the heart to embrace eternity of time and infinity of space in its every palpitation; it makes us live in the world as if walking in the garden of Eden; and all these spiritual feats are accomplished without resorting to any doctrines but by simply asserting in the most direct way the truth that lies in our inner being.

Whatever else Zen may be, it is practical and commonplace and at the same time most living. An ancient master, wishing to show what Zen is, lifted one of his fingers, another kicked a ball, and a third slapped the face of his questioner. If the inner truth that lies deep in us is thus demonstrated, is not Zen the most

45

practical and direct method of spiritual training ever resorted to by any religion? And is not this practical method also a most original one? Indeed, Zen cannot be anything else but original and creative because it refuses to deal with concepts but deals with living facts of life. When conceptually understood, the lifting of a finger is one of the most ordinary incidents in everybody's life. But when it is viewed from the Zen point of view it vibrates with divine meaning and creative vitality. So long as Zen can point out this truth in the midst of our conventional and concept-bound existence we must say that it has its reason of being.

The following quotation from a letter of Yengo (Yuan-wu in C. 1566–1642) may answer, to a certain extent, the question asked in the beginning of this chapter, "What is Zen?"

"It is presented right to your face, and at this moment the whole thing is handed over to you. For an intelligent fellow, one word should suffice to convince him of the truth of it, but even then error has crept in. Much more so when it is committed to paper and ink, or given up to wordy demonstration or to logical quibble, then it slips farther away from you. The great truth of Zen is possessed by everybody. Look into your own being and seek it not through others. Your own mind is above all forms; it is free and quiet and sufficient; it eternally stamps itself in your six senses and four elements. In its light all is absorbed. Hush the dualism of subject and object, forget both, transcend the intellect, sever yourself from the understanding, and directly penetrate deep into the identity of the Buddha-mind; outside of this there are no realities. Therefore, when Bodhidharma came from the West, he simply declared, 'Directly pointing to one's own soul, my doctrine is unique, and is not hampered by the canonical teachings; it is the absolute transmission of the true seal.' Zen has nothing to do with letters, words, or sutras. It only requests you to grasp the point directly and therein to find your peaceful abode. When the mind is disturbed, the understanding is stirred, things are recognized, notions are entertained, ghostly spirits are conjured, and prejudices grow rampant. Zen will then forever be lost in the maze.

"The wise Sekiso (Shih-shuang) said, 'Stop all your hankerings; let the mildew grow on your lips; make yourself like unto a perfect piece of immaculate silk; let your one thought be

46

eternity; let yourself be like dead ashes, cold and lifeless; again let yourself be like an old censer in a deserted village shrine!'

"Putting your simple faith in this, discipline yourself accordingly; let your body and mind be turned into an inanimate object of nature like a stone or a piece of wood; when a state of perfect motionlessness and unawareness is obtained all the signs of life will depart and also every trace of limitation will vanish. Not a single idea will disturb your consciousness, when lo! all of a sudden you will come to realize a light abounding in full gladness. It is like coming across a light in thick darkness; it is like receiving treasure in poverty. The four elements and the five aggregates are no more felt as burdens; so light, so easy, so free you are. Your very existence has been delivered from all limitations; you have become open, light, and transparent. You gain an illuminating insight into the very nature of things, which now appear to you as so many fairylike flowers having no graspable realities. Here is manifested the unsophisticated self which is the original face of your being; here is shown all bare the most beautiful landscape of your birthplace. There is but one straight passage open and unobstructed through and through. This is so when you surrender all—your body, your life, and all that belongs to your inmost self. This is where you gain peace, ease, non-doing, and inexpressible delight. All the sutras and sastras are no more than communications of this fact; all the sages, ancient as well as modern, have exhausted their ingenuity and imagination to no other purpose than to point the way to this. It is like unlocking the door to a treasury; when the entrance is once gained, every object coming into your view is yours, every opportunity that presents itself is available for your use; for are they not, however multitudinous, all possessions obtainable within the original being of yourself? Every treasure there is but waiting your pleasure and utilization. This is what is meant by 'Once gained, eternally gained, even unto the end of time.' Yet really there is nothing gained; what you have gained is no gain, and yet there is something truly gained in this."

III

IS ZEN NIHILISTIC?

In the history of Zen, Yeno (Hui-neng,[1] 638–713), traditionally considered the Sixth Patriarch of the Zen sect in China, cuts a most important figure. In fact, he is the founder of Zen as distinguished from the other Buddhist sects then existing in China. The standard set up by him as the true expression of Zen faith is this stanza:

> The Bodhi (True Wisdom) is not like the tree;
> The mirror bright is nowhere shining:
> As there is nothing from the first,
> Where does the dust itself collect?

This was written in answer to a stanza composed by another Zen monk who claimed to have understood the faith in its purity. His lines run thus:

> This body is the Bodhi-tree;
> The soul is like the mirror bright;
> Take heed to keep it always clean,
> And let no dust collect upon it.

They were both the disciples of the Fifth Patriarch, Gunin (Hung-jen, died 675); and he thought that Yeno rightly comprehended the spirit of Zen, and, therefore, was worthy of wearing his mantle and carrying his bowl as his true successor in Zen. This recognition by the master of the signification of the first stanza by Yeno stamps it as the orthodox expression of Zen faith. As it seems to breathe the spirit of nothingness, many people regard Zen as advocating nihilism. The purpose of the present chapter is to refute this.

It is true there are many passages in Zen literature which may be construed as conveying a nihilistic doctrine; for example, the

---

[1] Hui-neng is pronounced Wei-lang in Shanghai dialect.

48

theory of Sunyata (emptiness).[1] Even among those scholars who are well acquainted with the general teaching of Mahayana Buddhism, some still cling to the view that Zen is the practical application of the "Sanron" (san-lun) philosophy, otherwise known as the Madhyamika school. Sanron means the "three treatises", which are Nagarjuna's Madhyamika Sastra and The Discourse of Twelve Sections, and Deva's Discourse of One Hundred Stanzas. They comprise all the essential doctrines of this school. Nagarjuna is thought to be its founder, and as the Mahayana sutras classified under the head of Prajnaparamita expound more or less similar views, the philosophy of this school is sometimes designated as the Prajna doctrine. Zen, therefore, they think, practically belongs to this class; in other words, the ultimate signification of Zen would be the upholding of the Sunyata system.

To a certain extent, superficially at least, this view is justifiable. For instance, read the following:

"I come here to seek the truth of Buddhism," a disciple asked a master.

"Why do you seek such a thing here?" answered the master. "Why do you wander about, neglecting your own precious treasure at home? I have nothing to give you, and what truth of Buddhism do you desire to find in my monastery? There is nothing, absolutely nothing."

A master would sometimes say: "I do not understand Zen. I have nothing here to demonstrate; therefore, do not remain standing so, expecting to get something out of nothing. Get enlightened by yourself, if you will. If there is anything to take hold of, take it by yourself."

Again: "True knowledge (bodhi) transcends all modes of expression. There has been nothing from the very beginning which one can claim as having attained towards enlightenment."

Or: "In Zen there is nothing to explain by means of words, there is nothing to be given out as a holy doctrine. Thirty blows whether you affirm or negate. Do not remain silent; nor be discursive."

[1] What the theory of Sunyata really means is explained somewhat in detail in my Essays in Zen Buddhism, Series III, under "The Philosophy and Religion of the Prajnaparamita-Sutra" (pp. 207–88).

The question "How can one always be with Buddha?" called forth the following answer from a master: "Have no stirrings in your mind; be perfectly serene toward the objective world. To remain thus all the time in absolute emptiness and calmness is the way to be with the Buddha."

Sometimes we come across the following: "The middle way is where there is neither middle nor two sides. When you are fettered by the objective world, you have one side; when you are disturbed in your own mind, you have the other side. When neither of these exists, there is no middle part, and this is the middle way."

A Japanese Zen master who flourished several hundred years ago used to say to his disciples, who would implore him to instruct them in the way to escape the fetters of birth-and-death, "Here is no birth-and-death."

Bodhidharma (Daruma, J.; Tamo, C.), the First Patriarch of the Zen sect in China, was asked by Wu, the first Emperor (reigned A.D. 502–549) of the Liang dynasty, as to the ultimate and holiest principle of Buddhism. The sage is reported to have answered, "Vast emptiness and nothing holy in it."

These are passages taken at random from the vast store of Zen literature, and they seem to be permeated with the ideas of emptiness (*sunyata*), nothingness (*nasti*), quietude (*santi*), no-thought (*acinta*), and other similar notions, all of which we may regard as nihilistic or as advocating negative quietism.

A quotation from the *Prajnaparamita-Hridaya Sutra*[1] may prove to be more astounding than any of the above passages. In fact, all the sutras belonging to this Prajna class of Mahayana literature are imbued thoroughly with the idea of Sunyata, and those who are not familiar with this way of thinking will be taken aback and may not know how to express their judgment. This sutra, considered to be the most concise and most comprehensive of all the Prajna sutras, is daily recited in the Zen monasteries; in fact it is the first thing the monks recite in the morning as well as before each meal.

[1] See also the quotation from Sekiso, *supra*, often misunderstood as expressly advocating the doctrine of annihilation. For the original Sanskrit, Hsuan-chuang's Chinese translation, and a more literary and accurate English rendering, see my *Zen Essays*, Series III, pp. 190–206, where the author gives his own interpretation of the signification of this important sutra.

"Thus, Sariputra, all things have the character of emptiness, they have no beginning, no end, they are faultless and not faultless, they are not perfect and not imperfect. Therefore, O Sariputra, here in this emptiness there is no form, no perception, no name, no concepts, no knowledge. No eye, no ear, no nose, no tongue, no body, no mind. No form, no sound, no smell, no taste, no touch, no objects. . . . There is no knowledge, no ignorance, no destruction of ignorance. . . . There is no decay nor death; there are no four truths, viz. there is no pain, no origin of pain, no stoppage of pain, and no path to the stoppage of pain. There is no knowledge of Nirvana, no obtaining of it, no not-obtaining of it. Therefore, O Sariputra, as there is no obtaining of Nirvana, a man who has approached the Prajnaparamita of the Bodhisattvas dwells unimpeded in consciousness. When the impediments of consciousness are annihilated, then he becomes free of all fear, is beyond the reach of change, enjoying final Nirvana."

Going through all these quotations, it may be thought that the critics are justified in charging Zen with advocating a philosophy of pure negation, but nothing is so far from Zen as this criticism would imply. For Zen always aims at grasping the central fact of life, which can never be brought to the dissecting table of the intellect. To grasp this central fact of life, Zen is forced to propose a series of negations. Mere negation, however, is not the spirit of Zen, but as we are so accustomed to the dualistic way of thinking, this intellectual error must be cut at its root. Naturally Zen would proclaim, "Not this, not that, not anything." But we may insist upon asking Zen what it is that is left after all these denials, and the master will perhaps on such an occasion give us a slap in the face, exclaiming, "You fool, what is this?" Some may take this as only an excuse to get away from the dilemma, or as having no more meaning than a practical example of ill-breeding. But when the spirit of Zen is grasped in its purity, it will be seen what a real thing that slap is. For here is no negation, no affirmation, but a plain fact, a pure experience, the very foundation of our being and thought. All the quietness and emptiness one might desire in the midst of most active mentation lies therein. Do not be carried away by anything outward or conventional. Zen must be seized with bare hands, with no gloves on

Zen is forced to resort to negation because of our innate ignorance (*avidya*), which tenaciously clings to the mind as wet clothes do to the body. "Ignorance"[1] is all very well as far as it goes, but it must not go out of its proper sphere. "Ignorance" is another name for logical dualism. White is snow and black is the raven. But these belong to the world and its ignorant way of talking. If we want to get to the very truth of things, we must see them from the point where this world has not yet been created, where the consciousness of this and that has not yet been awakened and where the mind is absorbed in its own identity, that is, in its serenity and emptiness. This is a world of negations but leading to a higher or absolute affirmation—an affirmation in the midst of negations. Snow is not white, the raven is not black, yet each in itself is white or black. This is where our everyday language fails to convey the exact meaning as conceived by Zen.

Apparently Zen negates; but it is always holding up before us something which indeed lies right before our own eyes; and if we do not pick it up by ourselves, it is our own fault. Most people, whose mental vision is darkened by the clouds of ignorance, pass it by and refuse to look at it. To them Zen is, indeed, nihilism just because they do not see it. When Obaku (Huang-po, died 850) was paying reverence to the Buddha in the sanctuary, a pupil of his approached and said, "When Zen says not to seek it through the Buddha, nor through the Dharma, nor through the Sangha, why do you bow to the Buddha as if wishing to get something by this pious act?"

"I do not seek it," answered the master, "through the Buddha, nor through the Dharma, nor through the Sangha; I just go on doing this act of piety to the Buddha."

The disciple grunted, "What is the use, anyway, of looking so sanctimonious?"

The master gave him a slap in the face, whereupon the disciple said, "How rude you are!"

"Do you know where you are," exclaimed the master; "here I have no time to consider for your sake what rudeness or politeness means." With this another slap was given.

Intelligent readers will see in this attitude of Obaku something he is anxious to communicate in spite of his apparent

---

[1] This may be regarded as corresponding to Heraclitus' *Enantiodromia*, the regulating function of antithesis.

brusqueness to his disciple. He forbids outwardly, and yet in the spirit he is affirming. This must be comprehended if Zen is to be at all understood.

The attitude of Zen towards the formal worship of God may be gleaned more clearly from Joshu's (Chao-chou, 778–897) remarks given to a monk who was bowing reverently before Buddha. When Joshu slapped the monk, the latter said, "Is it not a laudable thing to pay respect to Buddha?" "Yes," answered the master, "but it is better to go without even a laudable thing." Does this attitude savour of anything nihilistic and iconoclastic? Superficially, yes; but let us dive deep into the spirit of Joshu out of the depths of which this utterance comes, and we will find ourselves confronting an absolute affirmation quite beyond the ken of our discursive understanding.

Hakuin (1685–1768), the founder of modern Japanese Zen, while still a young monk eagerly bent on the mastery of Zen, had an interview with the venerable Shoju. Hakuin thought that he fully comprehended Zen and was proud of his attainment, and this interview with Shoju was in fact intended to be a demonstration of his own high understanding. Shoju asked him how much he knew of Zen. Hakuin answered disgustingly, "If there is anything I can lay my hand on, I will get it all out of me." So saying, he acted as if he were going to vomit. Shoju took firm hold of Hakuin's nose and said: "What is this? Have I not after all touched it?" Let our readers ponder with Hakuin over this interview and find out for themselves what is that something which is so realistically demonstrated by Shoju.

Zen is not all negation, leaving the mind all blank as if it were pure nothing; for that would be intellectual suicide. There is in Zen something self-assertive, which, however, being free and absolute, knows no limitations and refuses to be handled in abstraction. Zen is a live fact, it is not like an inorganic rock or like an empty space. To come into contact with this living fact— nay, to take hold of it in every phase of life—is the aim of all Zen discipline.

Nansen (Nan-chuan, 748–834) was once asked by Hyakujo (Pai-chang, 720–814), one of his brother monks, if there was anything he dared not talk about to others. The master answered, "Yes."

Whereupon the monk continued, "What then is this some-thing you do not talk about?"

The master's reply was, "It is neither mind, nor Buddha, nor matter."

This looks to be the doctrine of absolute emptiness, but even here again we observe a glimpse of something showing itself through the negation. Observe the further dialogue that took place between the two. The monk said:

"If so, you have already talked about it."

"I cannot do any better. What would you say?"

"I am not a great enlightened one," answered Hyakujo.

The master said, "Well, I have already said too much about it."

This state of inner consciousness, about which we cannot make any logical statement, must be realized before we can have any intelligent talk on Zen. Words are only an index to this state; through them we are enabled to get into its signification, but do not look to words for absolute guidance. Try to see first of all in what mental state the Zen masters are so acting. They are not carrying on all those seeming absurdities, or, as some might say, those silly trivialities, just to suit their capricious moods. They have a certain firm basis of truth obtained from a deep personal experience. There is in all their seemingly crazy performances a systematic demonstration of the most vital truth. When seen from this truth, even the moving of the whole universe is of no more account than the flying of a mosquito or the waving of a fan. The thing is to see one spirit working throughout all these, which is an absolute affirmation, with not a particle of nihilism in it.

A monk asked Joshu, "What would you say when I come to you with nothing?"

Joshu said, "Fling it down to the ground."

Protested the monk, "I said that I had nothing; what shall I let go?"

"If so, carry it away," was the retort of Joshu.

Joshu has thus plainly exposed the fruitlessness of a nihilistic philosophy. To reach the goal of Zen, even the idea of "having nothing" ought to be done away with. Buddha reveals himself when he is no more asserted; that is, for Buddha's sake Buddha is to be given up. This is the only way to come to the realization of the truth of Zen. So long as one is talking of nothingness or of the absolute one is far away from Zen, and ever receding from Zen. Even the foothold of Sunyata must be kicked off. The only way to get saved is to throw oneself right down into a bottomless abyss. And this is, indeed, no easy task.

"No Buddhas," it is boldly asserted by Yengo (see p. 46), "have ever appeared on earth; nor is there anything that is to be given out as a holy doctrine. Bodhidharma, the First Patriarch of Zen, has never come east, nor has he ever transmitted any secret doctrine through the mind; only people of the world, not understanding what all this means, seek the truth outside of themselves. What a pity that the thing they are so earnestly looking for is being trodden under their own feet! This is not to be grasped by the wisdom of all the sages. However, we see the thing and yet it is not seen; we hear it and yet it is not heard; we talk about it and yet it is not talked about; we know it and yet it is not known. Let me ask, How does it so happen?"

Is this an interrogation as it apparently is? Or, in fact, is it an affirmative statement describing a certain definite attitude of mind?

Therefore, when Zen denies, it is not necessarily a denial in the logical sense. The same can be said of an affirmation. The idea is that the ultimate fact of experience must not be enslaved by any artificial or schematic laws of thought, nor by any antithesis of "yes" and "no", nor by any cut and dried formulae of epistemology. Evidently Zen commits absurdities and irrationalities all the time; but this only apparently. No wonder it fails to escape the natural consequences—misunderstandings, wrong interpretations, and ridicules which are often malicious. The charge of nihilism is only one of these.

When Vimalakirti asked Manjusri what was the doctrine of non-duality as realized by a Bodhisattva, Manjusri replied: "As I understand it, the doctrine is realized when one looks upon all things as beyond every form of expression and demonstration and as transcending knowledge and argument. This is my comprehension; may I ask what is your understanding?" Vimalakirti, thus demanded, remained altogether silent. The mystic response—that is, the closing of the lips—seems to be the only way one can get out of the difficulties in which Zen often finds itself involved,

55

when it is pressed hard for a statement. Therefore, Yengo (Yuan-wu), commenting on the above, has this to say:

"I say, 'yes', and there is nothing about which this affirmation is made; I say, 'no', and there is nothing about which this is made. I stand above 'yes' and 'no', I forget what is gained and what is lost. There is just a state of absolute purity, a state of stark nakedness. Tell me what you have left behind and what you see before. A monk may come out of the assembly and say, 'I see the Buddha-hall and the temple gate before me, my sleeping cell and living room behind.' Has this man an inner eye opened? When you can discriminate him, I will admit that you really have had a personal interview with the ancient sages."

When silence does not avail, shall we say, after Yengo, "The gate of Heaven opens above, and an unquenched fire burns below"? Does this make clear the ultimate signification of Zen, as not choked by the dualism of "yes" and "no"? Indeed, so long as there remains the last trace of consciousness as to this and that, *meum et tuum*, none can come to a fuller realization of Zen, and the sages of old will appear as those with whom we have nothing in common. The inner treasure will remain forever unearthed.

A monk asked, "According to Vimalakirti, one who wishes for the Pure Land ought to have his mind purified; but what is the purified mind?" Answered the Zen master: "When the mind is absolutely pure, you have a purified mind, and a mind is said to be absolutely pure when it is above purity and impurity. You want to know how this is to be realized? Have your mind thoroughly void in all conditions, then you will have purity. But when this is attained, do not harbour any thought of it, or you get non-purity. Again, when this state of non-purity is attained, do not harbour any thought of it, and you are free of non-purity. This is absolute purity." Now, absolute purity is absolute affirmation, as it is above purity and non-purity and at the same time unifies them in a higher form of synthesis. There is no negation in this, nor any contradiction. What Zen aims at is to realize this form of unification in one's everyday life of actualities, and not to treat life as a sort of metaphysical exercise. In this light all Zen "Questions and Answers" (*Mondo*) are to be considered. There are no quibblings, no playing at words, no sophistry; Zen is the most serious concern in the world.

Let me conclude this chapter with the following quotation[1] from one of the earliest Zen writings. Doko (Tao-kwang), a Buddhist philosopher and a student of the Vijnaptimatra (absolute idealism), came to a Zen master and asked:

"With what frame of mind should one discipline oneself in the truth?"

Said the Zen master, "There is no mind to be framed, nor is there any truth in which to be disciplined."

"If there is no mind to be framed and no truth in which to be disciplined, why do you have a daily gathering of monks who are studying Zen and disciplining themselves in the truth?"

The master replied: "I have not an inch of space to spare, and where could I have a gathering of monks? I have no tongue, and how would it be possible for me to advise others to come to me?"

The philosopher then exclaimed, "How can you tell me a lie like that to my face?"

"When I have no tongue to advise others, is it possible for me to tell a lie?"

Said Doko despairingly, "I cannot follow your reasoning."

"Neither do I understand myself," concluded the Zen master.

[1] This is taken from a work by Daiju Yekai (Tai-chu Huihai), disciple of Baso (Ma-tsu, died 738). For other quotations see elsewhere.

IV

ILLOGICAL ZEN

Empty-handed I go, and behold the spade is
    in my hands;
I walk on foot, and yet on the back of an ox
    I am riding;
When I pass over the bridge,
Lo, the water floweth not, but the bridge doth
    flow.

THIS is the famous gatha of Jenye (Shan-hui, A.D. 497–469),
who is commonly known as Fudaishi (Fu-tai-shih) and it summarily gives the point of view as entertained by the followers of
Zen. Though it by no means exhausts all that Zen teaches, it
indicates graphically the way toward which Zen tends. Those
who desire to gain an intellectual insight, if possible, into the truth
of Zen, must first understand what this stanza really means.

Nothing can be more illogical and contrary to common sense
than these four lines. The critic will be inclined to call Zen
absurd, confusing, and beyond the ken of ordinary reasoning.
But Zen is inflexible and would protest that the so-called common-
sense way of looking at things is not final, and that the reason
why we cannot attain to a thoroughgoing comprehension of the
truth is due to our unreasonable adherence to a "logical" interpretation of things. If we really want to get to the bottom of life,
we must abandon our cherished syllogisms, we must acquire a
new way of observation whereby we can escape the tyranny of
logic and the one-sidedness of our everyday phraseology. However paradoxical it may seem, Zen insists that the spade must be
held in your empty hands, and that it is not the water but the
bridge that is flowing under your feet.

These are not, however, the only irrational statements Zen
makes. There are many more equally staggering ones. Some may
declare Zen irrevocably insane or silly. Indeed, what would our
readers say to such assertions as the following?

58

"When Tom drinks, Dick gets tipsy."

"Who is the teacher of all the Buddhas, past, present, and future? John the cook."

"Last night a wooden horse neighed and a stone man cut capers."

"Lo, a cloud of dust is rising from the ocean, and the roaring of the waves is heard over the land."

Sometimes Zen will ask you such questions as the following:

"It is pouring now; how would you stop it?"

"When both hands are clapped a sound is produced: listen to the sound of one hand."

"If you have heard the sound of one hand, can you make me hear it too?"

"When we see about us mountains towering high and seas filling hollow places, why do we read in the sacred sutras that the Dharma is sameness, and there is nothing high, nothing low?"

Have the followers of Zen lost their senses? Or are they given up to deliberate mystification? Have all these statements no inner meaning, no edifying signification except to produce confusion in our minds? What is Zen through these apparent trivialities and irrationalities really driving us to comprehend? The answer is simple. Zen wants us to acquire an entirely new point of view whereby to look into the mysteries of life and the secrets of nature. This is because Zen has come to the definite conclusion that the ordinary logical process of reasoning is powerless to give final satisfaction to our deepest spiritual needs.

We generally think that "A is A" is absolute, and that the proposition "A is not-A" or "A is B" is unthinkable. We have never been able to break through these conditions of the understanding; they have been too imposing. But now Zen declares that words are words and no more. When words cease to correspond with facts it is time for us to part with words and return to facts. As long as logic has its practical value it is to be made use of; but when it fails to work, or when it tries to go beyond its proper limits, we must cry, "Halt!" Ever since the awakening of consciousness we have endeavoured to solve the mysteries of being and to quench our thirst for logic through the dualism of "A" and "not-A"; that is, by calling a bridge a bridge, by making the water flow, and dust arise from the earth; but to our great

59

disappointment we have never been able to obtain peace of mind, perfect happiness, and a thorough understanding of life and the world. We have come, as it were, to the end of our wits. No further steps could we take which would lead us to a broader field of reality. The inmost agonies of the soul could not be expressed in words, when lo! light comes over our entire being. This is the beginning of Zen. For we now realize that "A is not-A" after all, that logic is onesided, that illogicality so-called is not in the last analysis necessarily illogical; what is superficially irrational has after all its own logic, which is in correspondence with the true state of things. "Empty-handed I go, and behold the spade is in my hands!" By this we are made perfectly happy, for strangely this contradiction is what we have been seeking for all the time ever since the dawning of the intellect. The dawning of the intellect did not mean the assertion of the intellect but the transcending of itself. The meaning of the proposition "A is A" is realized only when "A is not-A". To be itself is not to be itself —this is the logic of Zen, and satisfies all our aspirations.

"The flower is not red, the willow is not green." This is regarded by Zen devotees as most refreshingly satisfying. So long as we think logic final we are chained, we have no freedom of spirit, and the real facts of life are lost sight of. Now, however, we have the key to the whole situation; we are master of realities; words have given up their domination over us. If we are pleased to call a spade not a spade, we have the perfect right to do so; a spade need not always remain a spade; and, moreover, this, according to the Zen master, expresses more correctly the state of reality which refuses to be tied up to names.

This breaking up of the tyranny of name and logic is at the same time spiritual emancipation; for the soul is no longer divided against itself. By acquiring the intellectual freedom the soul is in full possession of itself; birth and death no longer torment it; for there are no such dualities anywhere; we live even through death. Hitherto we have been looking at things in their contradicting and differentiating aspect, and have assumed an attitude toward them in accordance with that view, that is, more or less antagonistic. But this has been revolutionized, we have at last attained the point where the world can be viewed, as it were, from within. Therefore, "the iron trees are in full bloom"; and "in the midst of pouring rain I am not wet". The soul is thus made whole, perfect, and filled with bliss.

Zen deals with facts and not with their logical, verbal, prejudiced, and lame representations. Direct simplicity is the soul of Zen; hence its vitality, freedom, and originality. Christianity speaks much of simplicity of heart, and so do other religions, but this does not always mean to be simple-hearted or to be a Simple Simon. In Zen it means not to get entangled in intellectual subtleties, not to be carried away by philosophical reasoning that is so often ingenuous and full of sophistry. It means, again, to recognize facts as facts and to know that words are words and nothing else. Zen often compares the mind to a mirror free from stains. To be simple, therefore, according to Zen, will be to keep this mirror always bright and pure and ready to reflect simply and absolutely whatever comes before it. The result will be to acknowledge a spade to be a spade and at the same time not to be a spade. To recognize the first only is a common-sense view, and there is no Zen until the second is also admitted along with the first. The common-sense view is flat and tame, whereas that of Zen is always original and stimulating. Each time Zen is asserted things get vitalized; there is an act of creation.

Zen thinks we are too much of slaves to words and logic. So long as we remain thus fettered we are miserable and go through untold suffering. But if we want to see something really worth knowing, that is conducive to our spiritual happiness, we must endeavour once for all to free ourselves from all conditions; we must see if we cannot gain a new point of view from which the world can be surveyed in its wholeness and life comprehended inwardly. This consideration has compelled one to plunge oneself deep into the abyss of the "Nameless" and take hold directly of the spirit as it is engaged in the business of creating the world. Here is no logic, no philosophizing; here is no twisting of facts to suit our artificial measures; here is no murdering of human nature in order to submit it to intellectual dissections; the one spirit stands face to face with the other spirit like two mirrors facing each other, and there is nothing to intervene between their mutual reflections.

In this sense Zen is pre-eminently practical. It has nothing to do with abstractions or with subtleties of dialectics. It seizes the spade lying in front of you, and holding it forth, makes the bold declaration, "I hold a spade, yet I hold it not." No reference is made to God or to the soul; there is no talk about the infinite or a life after death. This handling of a homely spade, a most ordinary thing to see about us, opens all the secrets we encounter in life. And nothing more is wanted. Why? Because Zen has now cleared up a new approach to the reality of things. When a humble flower in the crannied wall is understood, the whole universe and all things in it and out of it are understood. In Zen the spade is the key to the whole riddle. How fresh and full of life it is—the way Zen grapples with the knottiest questions of philosophy!

A noted Christian Father of the early Middle Ages once exclaimed: "O poor Aristotle! Thou who has discovered for the heretics the art of dialectics, the art of building up and destroying, the art of discussing all things and accomplishing nothing!" So much ado about nothing, indeed! See how philosophers of all ages contradict one another after spending all their logical acumen and analytical ingenuity on the so-called problems of science and knowledge. No wonder the same old wise man, wanting to put a stop once for all to all such profitless discussions, has boldly thrown the following bomb right into the midst of those sand-builders: "*Certum est quia impossibile est*"; or, more logically, "*Credo quia absurdum est.*" I believe because it is irrational; is this not an unqualified confirmation of Zen?

An old master brought out his stick before an assemblage of monks and said: "O monks, do you see this? If you see it, what is it you see? Would you say, 'It is a stick'? If you do you are ordinary people, you have no Zen. But if you say, 'We do not see any stick,' then I would say, 'Here I hold one, and how can you deny the fact?' " There is no trifling in Zen. Until you have a third eye opened to see into the inmost secret of things, you cannot be in the company of the ancient sages. What is this third eye that sees the stick and yet sees it not? Where does one get this illogical apprehension of things?

Zen says, "Buddha preached forty-nine years and yet his 'broad tongue' (*tanujihva*) never once moved." Can one talk without moving one's tongue? Why this absurdity? The explanation given by Gensha (Hsuan-sha, 831–908) follows: "All those piously inclined profess to bless others in every possible way; but when they come across three kinds of invalids, how would they treat them? The blind cannot see even if a stick or a mallet is produced; the deaf cannot hear however fine the preaching may be; and the dumb cannot talk however much they are urged to do so. But if these people severally suffering cannot somehow be benefited, what good is there after all in Buddhism?" The explanation does not seem to explain anything after all. Perhaps Butsugen's (Fo-yen) comment may throw more light on the subject. He said to his disciples: "You each have a pair of ears; what have you ever heard with them? You each have one tongue; what have you ever preached with it? Indeed, you have never talked, you have never heard, you have never seen. From whence then do all these forms, voices, odours, and tastes come?" (That is to say, where does this world come from?)

If this remark still leaves us where we were before, let us see whether Ummon (Yun-men, died 966), one of the greatest of Zen masters who ever lived, can help us. A monk came to Ummon and asked to be enlightened upon the above remark by Gensha. Ummon ordered him first to salute him in the formal way. When the monk stood up after prostrating himself on the ground, Ummon pushed him with his stick, and the monk stepped back. The master said, "You are not blind, then." He now told the monk to come forward, which he did. The master said, "You are not deaf, then." He finally asked the monk if he understood what all this was about, and the latter replied, "No, sir." Ummon then concluded, "You are not dumb, then."

With all these comments and gestures, are we still travelling through a *terra incognita*? If so, there is no other way but to go back to the beginning and repeat the stanza:

> Empty-handed I go, and behold the spade is
> in my hands;
> I walk on foot, and yet on the back of an ox
> I am riding;

A few more words: the reason why Zen is so vehement in its attack on logic, and why the present work treats first of the illogical aspect of Zen, is that logic has so pervasively entered into life as to make most of us conclude that logic is life and without it life has no significance. The map of life has been so definitely

63

and so thoroughly delineated by logic that what we have to do is simply to follow it, and that we ought not to think of violating the laws of thought, which are final. Such a general view of life has come to be held by most people, though I must say that in point of fact they are constantly violating what they think inviolable. That is to say, they are "holding a spade and yet not holding it", they are making the sum of two and two sometimes three, sometimes five; only they are not conscious of this fact and imagine that their lives are logically or mathematically regulated. Zen wishes to storm this citadel of topsy-turvydom and to show that we live psychologically or biologically and not logically.

In logic there is a trace of effort and pain; logic is self-conscious. So is ethics, which is the application of logic to the facts of life. An ethical man performs acts of service which are praise-worthy, but he is all the time conscious of them, and, moreover, he may often be thinking of some future reward. Hence we should say that his mind is tainted and not at all pure, however objectively or socially good his deeds are. Zen abhors this. Life is an art, and like perfect art it should be self-forgetting; there ought not to be any trace of effort or painful feeling. Life, according to Zen, ought to be lived as a bird flies through the air or as a fish swims in the water. As soon as there are signs of elaboration, a man is doomed, he is no more a free being. You are not living as you ought to live, you are suffering under the tyranny of circum-stances; you are feeling a constraint of some sort, and you lose your independence. Zen aims at preserving your vitality, your native freedom, and above all the completeness of your being. In other words, Zen wants to live from within. Not to be bound by rules, but to be creating one's own rules—this is the kind of life which Zen is trying to have us live. Hence its illogical, or rather superlogical, statements.

In one of his sermons a Zen master[1] declares: "The sutras preached by the Buddha during his lifetime are said to amount to five thousand and forty-eight fascicles; they include the doctrine of emptiness and the doctrine of being; there are teachings of immediate realization and of gradual development. Is this not an affirmation?

[1] Goso Hoyen (Fa-yen of Wu-tsu-shan).

"But, according to Yoka,[1] 'There are no sentient beings, there are no Buddhas; sages as numerous as the sands of the Ganges are but so many bubbles in the sea; sages and worthies of the past are like flashes of lightning.' Is this not a negation?

"O you, my disciples, if you say there is, you go against Yoka; if you say there is not, you contradict our old master Buddha. If he were with us, then how would he pass through the dilemma? If you know, however, just exactly where we are, we shall be interviewing Buddha in the morning and saluting him in the evening. If, on the other hand, you confess your ignorance, I will let you see into the secret. When I say there is not, this does not necessarily mean a negation; when I say there is, this also does not signify an affirmation. Turn eastward and look at the Western Land; face the south and the North Star is pointed out there!"

[1] Yung-chia in his "Song of Enlightenment".

V

ZEN A HIGHER AFFIRMATION

SHUZAN (Shou-shan, 926–992) once held up his *shippe*[1] to an assembly of his disciples and declared: "Call this a *shippe* and you assert; call it not a *shippe* and you negate. Now, do not assert nor negate, and what would you call it? Speak, speak!" One of the disciples came out of the ranks, took the *shippe* away from the master, and breaking it in two, exclaimed, "What is this?"

To those who are used to dealing with abstractions and high subjects this may appear to be quite a trivial matter, for what have they, deep learned philosophers, to do with an insignificant piece of bamboo? How does it concern those scholars who are absorbed in deep meditation, whether it is called a bamboo stick or not, whether it is broken, or thrown on the floor? But to the followers of Zen this declaration by Shuzan is pregnant with meaning. Let us really realize the state of his mind in which he proposed this question, and we have attained our first entrance into the realm of Zen. There were many Zen masters who followed Shuzan's example, and, holding forth their *shippe*, demanded of their pupils a satisfactory answer.

To speak in the abstract, which perhaps will be more acceptable to most readers, the idea is to reach a higher affirmation than the logical antithesis of assertion and denial. Ordinarily, we dare not go beyond an antithesis just because we imagine we cannot. Logic has so intimidated us that we shrink and shiver whenever its name is mentioned. The mind made to work, ever since the awakening of the intellect, under the strictest discipline of logical dualism, refuses to shake off its imaginary cangue. It has never occurred to us that it is possible for us to escape this self-imposed intellectual limitation; indeed, unless we break through the antithesis of "yes" and "no" we can never hope to live a real life of freedom. And the soul has always been crying

[1] A stick about one and a half feet long, made of split bamboo bound with ratan. To be pronounced *ship-pei*.

for it, forgetting that it is not after all so very difficult to reach a higher form of affirmation, where no contradicting distinctions obtain between negation and assertion. It is due to Zen that this higher affirmation has finally been reached by means of a stick of bamboo in the hand of the Zen master.

It goes without saying that this stick thus brought forward can be any one of myriads of things existing in this world of particulars. In this stick we find all possible existences and also all our possible experiences concentrated. When we know it—this homely piece of bamboo—we know the whole story in a most thoroughgoing manner. Holding it in my hand, I hold the whole universe. Whatever statement I make about it is also made of everything else. When one point is gained, all other points go with it. As the Avatamsaka (Kegon) philosophy teaches: "The One embraces All, and All is merged in the One. The One is All, and All is the One. The One pervades All, and All is in the One. This is so with every object, with every existence." But, mind you, here is no pantheism, nor the theory of identity. For when the stick of bamboo is held out before you it is just the stick, there is no universe epitomized in it, no All, no One; even when it is stated that "I see the stick" or that "Here is a stick," we all miss the mark. Zen is no more there, much less the philosophy of the Avatamsaka.

I spoke of the illogicalness of Zen in one of the preceding chapters; the reader will now know why Zen stands in opposition to logic, formal or informal. It is not the object of Zen to look illogical for its own sake, but to make people know that logical consistency is not final, and that there is a certain transcendental statement that cannot be attained by mere intellectual cleverness. The intellectual groove of "yes" and "no" is quite accommodating when things run their regular course; but as soon as the ultimate question of life comes up, the intellect fails to answer it satisfactorily. When we say "yes", we assert, and by asserting we limit ourselves. When we say "no", we deny, and to deny is exclusion. Exclusion and limitation, which after all are the same thing, murder the soul; for is it not the life of the soul that lives in perfect freedom and in perfect unity? There is no freedom or unity in exclusion or in limitation. Zen is well aware of this. In accordance with the demands of our inner life, therefore, Zen takes us to an absolute realm wherein there are no antitheses of any sort.

We must remember, however, that we live in affirmation and not in negation, for life is affirmation itself; and this affirmation must not be the one accompanied or conditioned by a negation; such an affirmation is relative and not at all absolute. With such an affirmation life loses its creative originality and turns into a mechanical process grinding forth nothing but soulless flesh and bones. To be free, life must be an absolute affirmation. It must transcend all possible conditions, limitations, and antitheses that hinder its free activity. When Shuzan held forth his stick of bamboo, what he wanted of his disciples was for them to understand and realize this form of absolute affirmation. Any answer is satisfactory if it flows out of one's inmost being, for such is always an absolute affirmation. Therefore, Zen does not mean a mere escape from intellectual imprisonment, which sometimes ends in sheer wantonness. There is something in Zen that frees us from conditions and at the same time gives us a certain firm foothold, which, however, is not a foothold in a relative sense. The Zen master endeavours to take away all footholds from the disciple which he has ever had since his first appearance on earth, and then to supply him with one that is really no foothold. If the stick of bamboo is not to the purpose, anything that comes handy will be made use of. Nihilism is not Zen, for this bamboo stick or anything else cannot be done away with as words and logic can. This is the point we must not overlook in the study of Zen.

Some examples will be given for illustration. Toku-san (Teh-shan, 780–865) used to swing his big stick whenever he came out to preach in the hall, saying, "If you utter a word I will give you thirty blows; if you utter not a word, just the same, thirty blows on your head." This was all he would say to his disciples. No lengthy talk on religion or morality; no abstract discourse, no hair-splitting metaphysics; on the contrary, quite rough-shod riding. To those who associate religion with pusillanimity and sanctimoniousness the Zen master must appear a terribly unpolished fellow. But when facts are handled as facts, without any intermediary, they are generally rude things. We must squarely face them, for no amount of winking or evading will be of any avail. The inner eye is to be opened under a shower of thirty blows. An absolute affirmation must rise from the fiery crater of life itself.

Hoyen (Fa-yen, died 1104), of Gosozan (Wu-tsu-shan), once asked, "When you meet a wise man on your way, if you do not speak to him or remain silent, how would you interview him?" The point is to make one realize what I call an absolute affirmation. Not merely to escape the antithesis of "yes" and "no", but to find a positive way in which the opposites are perfectly harmonized—this is what is aimed at in this question. A master once pointed to a live charcoal and said to his disciples, "I call this fire, but you call it not so; tell me what it is." The same thing here again. The master intends to free his disciples' minds from the bondage of logic, which has ever been the bane of humanity.

This ought not to be regarded as a riddle proposed to puzzle you. There is nothing playful about it; if you fail to answer, you are to face the consequences. Are you going to be eternally chained by your own laws of thought, or are you going to be perfectly free in an assertion of life which knows no beginning or end? You cannot hesitate. Grasp the fact or let it slip—between these there is no choice. The Zen method of discipline generally consists in putting one in a dilemma, out of which one must contrive to escape, not through logic indeed, but through a mind of higher order.

Yakusan (Yueh-shan, 751–834) studied Zen first under Sekito (Shih-t'ou, 700–790) and asked him: "As to the three divisions and twelve departments of Buddhism, I am not altogether unacquainted with them, but I have no knowledge whatever concerning the doctrine of Zen as taught in the South.[1] Its followers assert it to be the doctrine of directly pointing at the mind and attaining Buddhahood through a perception of its real nature. If this is so, how may I be enlightened?" Sekito replied: "Assertion prevails not, nor does denial. When neither of them is to the point, what would you say?" Yakusan remained meditative, as he did not grasp the meaning of the question. The master then told him to go to Badaishi (Ma Tai-shih) of Chiang-hsi, who might be able to open the monk's eye to the truth of Zen. Thereupon, the monk Yakusan went to the new teacher with the

[1] Zen, in contradistinction to the other Buddhist schools, originated in the southern provinces of China.

same problem. His answer was, "I sometimes make one raise the eyebrows, or wink, while at other times to do so is altogether wrong." Yakusan at once comprehended the ultimate purport of this remark. When Baso asked, "What makes you come to this?" Yakusan replied, "When I was with Sekito, it was like a mosquito biting at an iron bull." Was this a satisfactory reason or explanation? How strange this so-called affirmation!

Riko (Li K'u), a high government officer of the T'ang dynasty, asked Nansen (Nan-chuan): "A long time ago a man kept a goose in a bottle. It grew larger and larger until it could not get out of the bottle any more; he did not want to break the bottle, nor did he wish to hurt the goose; how would you get it out?" The master called out, "O Officer!"—to which Riko at once responded, "Yes!" "There, it is out!" This was the way Nansen produced the goose out of its imprisonment. Did Riko get his higher affirmation?

Kyogen (Hsiang-yen)[1] said: "Suppose a man climbing up a tree takes hold of a branch by his teeth, and his whole body is thus suspended. His hands are not holding anything and his feet are off the ground. Now another man comes along and asks the man in the tree as to the fundamental principle of Buddhism. If the man in the tree does not answer, he is neglecting the questioner; but if he tries to answer he will lose his life; how can he get out of his predicament?" While this is put in the form of a fable its purport is like those already mentioned. If you open your mouth trying to affirm or to negate, you are lost. Zen is no more there. But merely remaining silent will not do, either. A stone lying there is silent, a flower in bloom under the window is silent, but neither of them understands Zen. There must be a certain way in which silence and eloquence become identical, that is, where negation and assertion are unified in a higher form of statement. When we attain to this we know Zen.

What, then, is an absolute affirmative statement? When Hyakujo (Pai-chang, 720-814) wished to decide who would be the next chief of Tai-kuei-shan monastery, he called in two of his chief disciples, and producing a pitcher, which a Buddhist monk generally carries about him, said to them, "Do not call it a pitcher

---

[1] A younger contemporary of Kuei-shan (771-853).

ZEN A HIGHER AFFIRMATION

but tell me what it is." The first one replied, "It cannot be called a piece of wood." The Abbot did not consider the reply quite to the mark; thereupon the second one came forward, lightly pushed the pitcher down, and without making any remark quietly left the room. He was chosen to be the new abbot, who afterwards became "the master of one thousand and five hundred monks". Was this upsetting a pitcher an absolute affirmation? You may repeat this act, but you will not necessarily be regarded as understanding Zen.

Zen abhors repetition or imitation of any kind, for it kills. For the same reason Zen never explains, but only affirms. Life is fact and no explanation is necessary or pertinent. To explain is to apologize, and why should we apologize for living? To live—is that not enough? Let us then live, let us affirm! Herein lies Zen in all its purity and in all its nudity as well.

In the monastery of Nansen monks of the eastern wing quarrelled with those of the western wing over the possession of a cat. The master seized it and lifting it before the disputing monks, said, "If any of you can say something to save the poor animal, I will let it go." As nobody came forward to utter a word of affirmation, Nansen cut the object of dispute in two, thus putting an end forever to an unproductive quarrelling over "yours" and "mine". Later on Joshu (Chao-chou) came back from an outing and Nansen put the case before him, and asked him what he would have done to save the animal. Joshu without further ado took off his straw sandals and, putting them on his head, went out. Seeing this, Nansen said, "If you were here at the time you would have saved the cat."

What does all this mean? Why was a poor innocent creature sacrificed? What has Joshu's placing his sandals over his head to do with the quarrelling? Did Nansen mean to be irreligious and inhuman by killing a living being? Was Joshu really a fool to play such a strange trick? And then "absolute denial" and "absolute affirmation"—are these really two? There is something fearfully earnest in both these actors, Joshu and Nansen. Unless this is apprehended, Zen is, indeed, a mere farce. The cat certainly was not killed to no purpose. If any of the lower animals is ever to attain Buddhahood, this cat was surely the one so destined.

The same Joshu was once asked by a monk, "All things are reducible to the One; where is this One to be reduced?" The master's reply was, "When I was in Tsin district I had a monk's robe made that weighed seven *chin*." This is one of the most noted sayings ever uttered by a Zen master. One may ask: "Is this what is meant by an absolute affirmation? What possible connection is there between a monk's robe and the oneness of things?" Let me ask: You believe that all things exist in God, but where is the abode of God? Is it in Joshu's seven-*chin* cassock? When you say that God is here, he can no more be there; but you cannot say that he is nowhere, for by your definition God is omnipresent. So long as we are fettered by the intellect, we cannot interview God as he is; we seek him everywhere, but he ever flies away from us. The intellect desires to have him located, but it is in his very nature that he cannot be limited. Here is a great dilemma to put to the intellect, and it is an inevitable one. How shall we find the way out? Joshu's priestly robe is not ours; his way of solution cannot be blindly followed, for each of us must beat out his own track. If someone comes to you with the same question, how will you answer it? And are we not at every turn of life confronted with the same problem? And is it not ever pressing for an immediate and most practical solution?

Gutei's (Chu-chih)[1] favourite response to any question put to him was to lift one of his fingers. His little boy attendant imitated him, and whenever the boy was asked by strangers as to the teaching of the master he would lift his finger. Learning of this, the master one day called the boy in and cut off his finger. The boy in fright and pain tried to run away, but was called back, when the master held up his finger. The boy tried to imitate the master, as was his wont, but the finger was no more there, and then suddenly the significance of it all dawned upon him. Copying is slavery. The letter must never be followed, only the spirit is to be grasped. Higher affirmations live in the spirit. And where is the spirit? Seek it in your everyday experience, and therein lies abundance of proof for all you need.

We read in a sutra: "There was an old woman on the east side of the town who was born when the Buddha was born, and they lived in the same place throughout all their lives. The old

[1] A disciple of T'ien-lung, of the ninth century.

woman did not wish to see the Buddha; if he ever approached she tried in every way to avoid him, running up and down, hiding herself hither and thither. But one day, finding it impossible to flee from him, she covered her face with her hands, and lo, the Buddha appeared between each of her ten fingers. Let me ask, 'Who is this old lady?' "

Absolute affirmation is the Buddha; you cannot fly away from it, for it confronts you at every turn; but somehow you do not recognize it until you, like Gutei's little boy, lose a finger. It is strange, but the fact remains that we are like "those who die of hunger while sitting beside the rice bag", or rather like "those who die of thirst while standing thoroughly drenched in the midst of the river". One master goes a step further and says that "We are the rice itself and the water itself." If so we cannot truthfully say that we are hungry or thirsty, for from the very beginning nothing has been wanting in us. A monk came to Sozan (T'sao-shan, 840-901) asking him to be charitable, as he was quite destitute. Sozan called out, "O my venerable sir!" to which the monk immediately responded. Then said Sozan, "You have already had three big bowlfuls of rich home-made *chu* (liquor), and yet you insist that it has never yet wetted your lips!" Perhaps we are all like this poor opulent monk; when we are already quite filled up, we never realize the fact.

To conclude, here is another of the innumerable statements that abound in Zen literature, absolutely affirming the truth of Zen. Seihei (Tsing-ping, 845-919) asked Suibi (T'sui-wei) :[1]

"What is the fundamental principle of Buddhism?"

"Wait," said Suibi; "when there is no one around I will tell you."

After a while Seihei repeated the request, saying, "There is no one here now; pray enlighten me."

Coming down from his chair, Suibi took the anxious inquirer into the bamboo grove, but said nothing. When the latter pressed for a reply, Suibi whispered: "How high these bamboos are! And how short those over there!"

---

[1] *The Transmission of the Lamp (Chuan-teng Lu)*, Vol. XV.

PRACTICAL ZEN

So far Zen has been discussed from the intellectual point of view, in order to see that it is impossible to comprehend Zen through this channel; in fact it is not doing justice to Zen to treat it thus philosophically. Zen abhors media, even the intellectual medium; it is primarily and ultimately a discipline and an experience, which is dependent on no explanation; for an explanation wastes time and energy and is never to the point; all that you get out of it is a misunderstanding and a twisted view of the thing. When Zen wants you to taste the sweetness of sugar, it will put the required article right into your mouth and no further words are said. The followers of Zen would say, A finger is needed to point at the moon, but what a calamity it would be if one took the finger for the moon! This seems improbable, but how many times we are committing this form of error we do not know. Ignorance alone often saves us from being disturbed in our self-complacency. The business of a writer on Zen, however, cannot go beyond the pointing at the moon, as this is the only means permitted to him in the circumstances; and everything that is within his power will be done to make the subject in hand as thoroughly comprehensible as it is capable of being so made. When Zen is metaphysically treated, the reader may get somewhat discouraged about its being at all intelligible, since most people are not generally addicted to speculation or introspection. Let me approach it from quite a different point, which is perhaps more genuinely Zen-like.

When Joshu (Chao-chou) was asked what the Tao (or the truth of Zen) was, he answered, "Your everyday life, that is the Tao." In other words, a quiet, self-confident, and trustful existence of your own—this is the truth of Zen, and what I mean when I say that Zen is pre-eminently practical. It appeals directly to life, not even making reference to a soul or to God, or to anything that interferes with or disturbs the ordinary course of living. The idea of Zen is to catch life as it flows. There is nothing extraordinary or mysterious about Zen. I raise my hand; I take a book from the other side of this desk; I hear the boys playing ball outside my window; I see the clouds blown away beyond the neighbouring woods:—in all these I am practising Zen, I am living Zen. No wordy discussion is necessary, nor any explanation. I do not know why—and there is no need of explaining, but when the sun rises the whole world dances with joy and everybody's heart is filled with bliss. If Zen is at all conceivable, it must be taken hold of here.

Therefore, when Bodhidharma (Daruma in J.; Ta-mo in C.) was asked who he was, he said, "I do not know." This was not because he could not explain himself, nor was it because he wanted to avoid any verbal controversy, but just because he did not know what or who he was, save that he was what he was and could not be anything else. The reason was simple enough. When Nangaku (Nan-yueh, 677-744) was approaching the Sixth Patriarch, and was questioned, "What is it that thus walks toward me?" he did not know what to answer. For eight long years he pondered the question, when one day it dawned upon him, and he exclaimed, "Even to say it is something does not hit the mark." This is the same as saying, "I do not know."

Sekito once asked his disciple, Yakusan (Yueh-shan), "What are you doing here?" "I am not doing anything," answered the latter. "If so you are idling your time away." "Is not idling away the time doing something?" was Yakusan's response. Sekito still pursued him. "You say you are not doing anything; who then is this one who is doing nothing?" Yakusan's reply was the same as that of Bodhidharma, "Even the wisest know it not." There is no agnosticism in it, nor mysticism either, if this is understood in the sense of mystification. A plain fact is stated here in plain language. If it does not seem so to the reader, it is because he has not attained to this state of mind which enabled Bodhidharma or Sekito to make the statement.

The Emperor Wu of the Liang dynasty requested Fu Daishi (Fu-ta-shih, 497-569) to discourse on a Buddhist sutra. The Daishi taking the chair sat solemnly in it but uttered not a word. The Emperor said, "I asked you to give a discourse, and why do

75

you not begin to speak?" Shih, one of the Emperor's attendants, said, "The Daishi has finished discoursing." What kind of a sermon did this silent Buddhist philosopher deliver? Later on, a Zen master commenting on the above says, "What an eloquent sermon it was!" Vimalakirti, the hero of the sutra bearing his name, had the same way of answering the question, "What is the absolute doctrine of non-duality?" Someone remarked, "Thundering, indeed, is this silence of Vimalakirti." Was this keeping the mouth closed really so deafening? If so, I hold my tongue now, and the whole universe, with all its hullabaloo and hurly-burly, is at once absorbed in this absolute silence. But mimicry does not turn a frog into a green leaf. Where there is no creative originality there is no Zen. I must say: "Too late, too late! The arrow has gone off the string."

A monk asked Yeno (Hui-neng), the Sixth Patriarch, "Who has inherited the spirit of the Fifth Patriarch (Hung-jen)?"

Answered Yeno, "One who understands Buddhism."

"Have you then inherited it?"

"No," replied Yeno, "I have not."

"Why have you not?" was naturally the next question of the monk.

"Because I do not understand Buddhism," Yeno reasoned.

How hard, then, and yet how easy it is to understand the truth of Zen! Hard because to understand it is not to understand it; easy because not to understand it is to understand it. A master declares that even Buddha Sakyamuni and Bodhisattva Maitreya do not understand it, where simple-minded knaves do understand it.

We can now see why Zen shuns abstractions, representations, and figures of speech. No real value is attached to such words as God, Buddha, the soul, the Infinite, the One, and suchlike words. They are, after all, only words and ideas, and as such are not conducive to the real understanding of Zen. On the contrary, they often falsify and play at cross purposes. We are thus compelled always to be on our guard. Said a Zen master, "Cleanse the mouth thoroughly when you utter the word Buddha." Or, "There is one word I do not like to hear; that is, Buddha." Or, "Pass quickly on where there is no Buddha, nor stay where he is." Why are the followers of Zen so antagonistic toward Buddha?

76

Is not Buddha their Lord? Is he not the highest reality of Buddhism? He cannot be such a hateful or unclean thing as to be avoided by Zen adherents. What they do not like is not the Buddha himself, but the odium attached to the word.

The answers given by Zen masters to the question "Who or what is the Buddha?" are full of varieties; and why so? One reason at least is that they thus desire to free our minds from all possible entanglements and attachments such as words, ideas, desires, etc., which are put up against us from the outside. Some of the answers are, then, as follows:

"One made of clay and decorated with gold."

"Even the finest artist cannot paint him."

"The one enshrined in the Buddha Hall."

"He is no Buddha."

"Your name is Yecho."

"The dirt-scraper all dried up."

"See the eastern mountains moving over the waves."

"No nonsense here."

"Surrounded by the mountains are we here."

"The bamboo grove at the foot of Chang-lin hill."

"Three pounds of flax."

"The mouth is the gate of woe."

"Lo, the waves are rolling over the plateau."

"See the three-legged donkey go trotting along."

"A reed has grown piercing through the leg."

"Here goes a man with the chest exposed and the legs all naked."

These are culled at random from a few books I am using for the purpose. When a thorough systematic search is made in the entire body of Zen literature we get quite a collection of the most strange statements ever made concerning such a simple question as, "Who is the Buddha?" Some of the answers given above are altogether irrelevant; they are, indeed, far from being appropriate so far as we judge them from our ordinary standard of reasoning. The others seem to be making sport of the question or of the questioner himself. Can the Zen masters who make such remarks be considered to be in earnest and really desiring the enlightenment of their followers? But the point is to have our minds work in complete union with the state of mind in which the masters uttered these strange words. When this is done, every one of these answers appears in an altogether new light and becomes wonderfully transparent.

Being practical and directly to the point, Zen never wastes time or words in explanation. Its answers are always curt and pithy; there is nothing circumlocutory in Zen; the master's words come out spontaneously and without a moment's delay. A gong is struck and its vibrations instantly follow. If we are not on the alert we fail to catch them; a mere winking and we miss the mark forever. They justly compare Zen to lightning. The rapidity, however, does not constitute Zen; its naturalness, its freedom from artificialities, its being expressive of life itself, its originality—these are the essential characteristics of Zen. Therefore, we have always to be on guard not to be carried away by outward signs when we really desire to get into the core of Zen. How difficult and how misleading it would be to try and understand Zen literally and logically, depending on those statements which have been given above as answers to the question "What is the Buddha?" Of course, so far as they are given as answers they are pointers by which we may know where to look for the presence of the Buddha; but we must remember that the finger pointing at the moon remains a finger and under no circumstances can it be changed into the moon itself. Danger always lurks where the intellect slyly creeps in and takes the index for the moon itself.

Yet there are philosophers who, taking some of the above utterances in their literary and logical sense, try to see something of pantheism in them. For instance, when the master says, "Three pounds of flax," or "A dirt-scraper," by this is apparently meant, they would insist, to convey a pantheistic idea. That is to say that those Zen masters consider the Buddha to be manifesting himself in everything: in the flax, in a piece of wood, in the running stream, in the towering mountains, or in works of art. Mahayana Buddhism, especially Zen, seems to indicate something of the spirit of pantheism, but nothing is in fact farther from Zen than this representation. The masters from the beginning have foreseen this dangerous tendency, and that is why they make those apparently incoherent statements. Their intention is to set the minds of their disciples or of scholars free from being oppressed by any fixed opinions or prejudices or so-called logical interpretations. When Tozan (Tung-shan, a disciple of Ummon) answered, "Three pounds of flax," to the question, "What is the Buddha?"—which, by the way, is the same thing as asking, "What is God?"—he did not mean that the flax he might have been handling at the time was a visible manifestation of Buddha, that Buddha when seen with an eye of intelligence could be met with in every object. His answer simply was, "Three pounds of flax." He did not imply anything metaphysical in this plain matter-of-fact utterance. These words came out of his inmost consciousness as water flows out of a spring, or as a bud bursts forth in the sun. There was no premeditation or philosophy on his part. Therefore, if we want to grasp the meaning of "Three pounds of flax," we first have to penetrate into the inmost recess of Tozan's consciousness and not to try to follow up his mouth. At another time he may give an entirely different answer, which might directly contradict the one already given. Logicians will naturally be nonplussed; they may declare him altogether out of mind. But the students of Zen will say, "It is raining so gently, see how fresh and green the grass is," and they know well that their answer is in full accord with Tozan's "Three pounds of flax."

The following will perhaps show further that Zen is not a form of pantheism, if we understand by this any philosophy that identifies the visible universe with the highest reality, called God, or Mind, or otherwise, and states that God cannot exist independent of his manifestations. In fact, Zen is something more than this. In Zen there is no place for time-wasting philosophical discussion. But philosophy is also a manifestation of life-activity, and therefore Zen does not necessarily shun it. When a philosopher comes to be enlightened, the Zen master is never loath to meet him on his own ground. The earlier Zen masters were comparatively tolerant toward the so-called philosophers and not so impatient as in the case of Rinzai (Lin-chi, died 867) or Tokusan (Te-shan, 780–865), whose dealings with them were swift and most direct. What follows is taken from a treatise by Daiju[1] on some principles of Zen compiled in the eighth (or

---

[1] Daiju Ekai, or Ta-chu Hui-hai in Chinese, was a disciple of Ma-tsu (died 788), and his work, which may be rendered "A Treatise on the Essence of Sudden Awakening", in two fascicles, gives the principal teachings of Zen as then understood.

79

ninth) century, when Zen had begun to flourish in all its bril-
liance and with all its uniqueness. A monk asked Daiju:

"Q. Are words the Mind?

"A. No, words are external conditions (*yen* in J.; *yuan* in C.);
they are not the Mind.

"Q. Apart from external conditions, where is the Mind to be
sought?

"A. There is no Mind independent of words. [That is to say,
the Mind is in words, but is not to be identified with them.]

"Q. If there is no Mind independent of words, what is the
Mind?

"A. The Mind is formless and imageless. The truth is, it is
neither independent of nor dependent upon words. It is eternally
serene and free in its activity. Says the Patriarch, 'When you
realize that the Mind is no Mind, you understand the Mind and
its workings.' "

Daiju further writes: "That which produces all things is
called Dharma-nature, or Dharmakaya. By the so-called Dharma
is meant the Mind of all beings. When this Mind is stirred up, all
things are stirred up. When the Mind is not stirred up, there is
nothing stirring and there is no name. The confused do not
understand that the Dharmakaya, in itself formless, assumes
individual forms according to conditions. The confused take the
green bamboo for Dharmakaya itself, the yellow blooming tree
for Prajna itself. But if the tree were Prajna, Prajna would be
identical with the non-sentient. If the bamboo were Dharmakaya,
Dharmakaya would be identical with a plant. But Dharmakaya
exists, Prajna exists, even when there is no blooming tree, no
green bamboo. Otherwise, when one eats a bamboo-shoot, this
would be eating up Dharmakaya itself. Such views as this are
really not worth talking about."

II

Those who have only read the foregoing treatment of Zen as
illogical, or of Zen as a higher affirmation, may conclude that
Zen is something unapproachable, something far apart from our
ordinary everyday life, something very alluring but very elusive;

and we cannot blame them for so thinking. Zen ought, therefore, to be presented also from its easy, familiar, and approachable side. Life is the basis of all things; apart from it nothing can stand. With all our philosophy, with all our grand and enhancing ideas, we cannot escape life as we live it. Star-gazers are still walking on the solid earth.

What is Zen, then, when made accessible to everybody? Joshu (Chao-chou) once asked a new monk:

"Have you ever been here before?"

The monk answered, "Yes, sir, I have."

Thereupon the master said, "Have a cup of tea."

Later on another monk came and he asked him the same question, "Have you ever been here?"

This time the answer was quite opposite. "I have never been here, sir."

The old master, however, answered just as before, "Have a cup of tea."

Afterwards the Inju (the managing monk of the monastery) asked the master, "How is it that you make the same offering of a cup of tea no matter what a monk's reply is?"

The old master called out, "O Inju!" who at once replied, "Yes, master." Whereupon Joshu said, "Have a cup of tea."

Joshu (778–897) was one of the most astute Zen masters during the T'ang dynasty, and the development of Zen in China owes much to him. He is said to have travelled even when he was eighty years of age, his object being to perfect himself in the mastery of Zen. He died in his one hundred and twentieth year. Whatever utterances he made were like jewels that sparkled brightly. It was said of him, "His Zen shines upon his lips." A monk who was still a novice came to him and asked to be instructed in Zen.

Joshu said, "Have you not had your breakfast yet?"

Replied the monk, "Yes, sir, I have had it already."

"If so, wash your dishes." This remark by the old master opened the novice's eye to the truth of Zen.

One day he was sweeping the ground when a monk asked him, "You are such a wise and holy master; tell me how it is that dust ever accumulates in your yard."

Said the master, "It comes from the outside."

Another time he was asked, "Why does this holy place attract dust?" To which his reply was, "There, another particle of dust!"

There was a famous stone bridge at Joshu's monastery, which was one of the sights there. A stranger monk inquired of him, "I have for some time heard of your famous stone bridge, but I see no such thing here, only a plank."

Said Joshu, "You see a plank and don't see a stone bridge."

"Where then is the stone bridge?"

"You have just crossed it," was the prompt reply.

At another time when Joshu was asked about this same stone bridge, his answer was, "Horses pass it, people pass it, everybody passes it."

In these dialogues do we only see trivial talks about ordinary things of life and nature? Is there nothing spiritual, conducive to the enlightenment of the religious soul? Is Zen, then, too practical, too commonplace? Is it too abrupt a descent from the height of transcendentalism to everyday things? Well, it all depends on how you look at it. A stick of incense is burning on my desk. Is this a trivial affair? An earthquake shakes the earth and Mt. Fuji topples over. Is this a great event? Yes, so long as the conception of space remains. But are we really living confined within an enclosure called space? Zen would answer at once: "With the burning of an incense-stick the whole *triloka* burns. Within Joshu's cup of tea the mermaids are dancing." So long as one is conscious of space and time, Zen will keep a respectable distance from you; your holiday is ill-spent, your sleep is disturbed, and your whole life is a failure.

Read the following dialogue between Yisan (Kuei-shan) and Kyozan (Yang-shan). At the end of his summer's sojourn Kyozan paid a visit to Yisan, who said, "I have not seen you this whole summer coming up this way; what have you been doing down there?"

Replied Kyozan, "Down there I have been tilling a piece of ground and finished sowing millet seeds."

Yisan said, "Then you have not wasted your summer."

It was now Kyozan's turn to ask Yisan as to his doings during the past summer, and he asked, "How did you pass your summer?"

"One meal a day and a good sleep at night."

This brought out Kyozan's comment, "Then you have not wasted your summer."

A Confucian scholar writes, "They seek the truth too far away from themselves, while it is right near them." The same thing may be said of Zen. We look for its secrets where they are most unlikely to be found, that is, in verbal abstractions and metaphysical subtleties, whereas the truth of Zen really lies in the concrete things of our daily life. A monk asked the master: "It is some time since I came to you to be instructed in the holy path of the Buddha, but you have never given me even an inkling of it. I pray you to be more sympathetic." To this the following answer was given: "What do you mean, my son? Every morning you salute me, and do I not return it? When you bring me a cup of tea, do I not accept it and enjoy drinking it? Besides this, what more instructions do you desire from me?"

Is this Zen? Is this the kind of life-experience Zen wants us to have? A Zen poet sings:

> How wondrously strange, and how miraculous this!
> I draw water, I carry fuel.

When Zen is said to be illogical and irrational, timid readers are frightened and may wish to have nothing to do with it, but I am confident that the present chapter devoted to practical Zen will mitigate whatever harshness and uncouthness there may have been in it when it was intellectually treated. In so far as the truth of Zen is on its practical side and not in its irrationality, we must not put too much emphasis on its irrationality. This may tend only to make Zen more inaccessible to ordinary intellects, but in order to show further what a simple and matter-of-fact business Zen is, and at the same time to emphasize the practical side of Zen, I will cite some more of the so-called "cases" in which appeal is made to the most naïve experience one may have in life. Naïve they are, indeed, in the sense of being free from conceptual demonstration or from intellectual analysis. You see a stick raised, or you are asked to pass a piece of household furniture, or are simply addressed by your name. Such as these are the simplest incidents of life occurring every day and being passed without any particular notice, and yet Zen is there—the

Zen that is supposed to be so full of irrationalities, or, if you like to put it so, so full of the highest speculations that are possible to the human understanding. The following are some more of these instances, simple, direct, and practical, and yet pregnant with meaning.

Sekkyo (Shih-kung)[1] asked one of his accomplished monks, "Can you take hold of empty space?"

"Yes, sir," he replied.

"Show me how you do it."

The monk stretched out his arm and clutched at empty space.

Sekkyo said: "Is that the way? But after all you have not got anything."

"What then," asked the monk, "is your way?"

The master straightway took hold of the monk's nose and gave it a hard pull, which made the latter exclaim: "Oh, oh, how hard you pull at my nose! You are hurting me terribly!"

"That is the way to have good hold of empty space," said the master.

When Yenkwan (Yen-kuan), one of Ma-tsu's disciples, was asked by a monk who the real Vairochana Buddha was, he told the monk to pass over a water-pitcher which was near by. The monk brought it to him as requested, but Yenkwan now ordered it to be taken back to its former place. After obediently following the order, the monk again asked the master who the real Vairochana Buddha was. "The venerable old Buddha is no more here," was the reply. Concerning this incident another Zen master comments, "Yes, the venerable old Buddha has long been here."

If these incidents are regarded as not entirely free from intellectual complications, what would you think of the following case of Chu (Chung, died 775), the national teacher of Nan-yang, who used to call his attendant three times a day, saying, "O my attendant, my attendant!" To this the attendant would respond regularly, "Yes, master." Finally the master remarked, "I thought I was in the wrong with you, but it is you

[1] A disciple of Ma-tsu. He was a hunter before conversion, and for his interview with Ma-tsu see my Zen Essays, III, under "Shih-kung and San-ping", by Motonobu Kano.

that is in the wrong with me." Is this not simple enough?—just calling one by name? Chu's last comment may not be so very intelligible from an ordinary logical point of view, but one calling and another responding is one of the commonest and most practical affairs of life. Zen declares that the truth is precisely there, so we can see what a matter-of-fact thing Zen is. There is no mystery in it, the fact is open to all: I hail you, and you call back; one "hallo!" calls forth another "hallo!" and this is all there is to it.

Ryosui (Liang-sui) was studying Zen under Mayoku (Ma-ku, a contemporary of Rinzai), and when Mayoku called out, "O Ryosui!" he answered, "Yes!" Thus called three times, he answered three times, when the master remarked, "O you stupid fellow!" This brought Ryosui to his senses; he now understood Zen and exclaimed: "O master, don't deceive me any more. If I had not come to you I should have been miserably led astray all my life by the sutras and the sastras." Later on Ryosui said to some of his fellow-monks who had been spending their time in the mastery of Buddhist philosophy, "All that you know, I know; but what I know, none of you know." Is it not wonderful that Ryosui could make such an utterance just by understanding the significance of his master's call?

Do these examples make the subject in hand any clearer or more intelligible than before? I can multiply such instances indefinitely, but those so far cited may suffice to show that Zen is after all not a very complicated affair, or a study requiring the highest faculty of abstraction and speculation. The truth and power of Zen consists in its very simplicity, directness, and utmost practicalness. "Good morning; how are you today?" "Thank you, I am well"—here is Zen. "Please have a cup of tea"—this, again, is full of Zen. When a hungry monk at work heard the dinner-gong he immediately dropped his work and showed himself in the dining-room. The master, seeing him, laughed heartily, for the monk had been acting Zen to its fullest extent. Nothing could be more natural; the one thing needful is just to open one's eye to the significance of it all.

But here is a dangerous loophole which the student of Zen ought to be especially careful to avoid. Zen must never be confused with naturalism or libertinism, which means to follow one's natural bent without questioning its origin and value. There is a great difference between human action and that of the animals, which are lacking in moral intuition and religious consciousness. The animals do not know anything about exerting themselves in order to improve their conditions or to progress in the way to higher virtues. Sekkyo was one day working in the kitchen when Baso, his Zen teacher, came in and asked what he was doing. "I am herding the cow," said the pupil. "How do you attend her?" "If she goes out of the path even once, I pull her back straightway by the nose; not a moment's delay is allowed." Said the master, "You truly know how to take care of her." This is not naturalism. Here is an effort to do the right thing.

A distinguished teacher was once asked, "Do you ever make any effort to get disciplined in the truth?"

"Yes, I do."

"How do you exercise yourself?"

"When I am hungry I eat; when tired I sleep."

"This is what everybody does; can they be said to be exercising themselves in the same way as you do?"

"No."

"Why not?"

"Because when they eat they do not eat, but are thinking of various other things, thereby allowing themselves to be di turbed; when they sleep they do not sleep, but dream of a thousand and one things. This is why they are not like myself."

If Zen is to be called a form of naturalism, then it is so with a rigorous discipline at the back of it. It is in that sense, and not as it is understood by libertines, that Zen may be designated naturalism. The libertines have no freedom of will, they are bound hands and feet by external agencies before which they are utterly helpless. Zen, on the contrary, enjoys perfect freedom; that is, it is master of itself. Zen has no "abiding place", to use a favourite expression in the *Prajnaparamita Sutras*. When a thing has its fixed abode, it is fettered, it is no more absolute. The following dialogue will very clearly explain this point.

A monk asked, "Where is the abiding place for the mind?"

"The mind," answered the master, "abides where there is no abiding."

"What is meant by 'there is no abiding'?"

"When the mind is not abiding in any particular object, we say that it abides where there is no abiding."

"What is meant by not abiding in any particular object?"

"It means not to be abiding in the dualism of good and evil, being and non-being, thought and matter; it means not to be abiding in emptiness or in non-emptiness, neither in tranquillity nor in non-tranquillity. Where there is no abiding place, this is truly the abiding place for the mind."

Seppo (Hsueh-feng, 822–908) was one of the most earnest truth-seekers in the history of Zen during the T'ang dynasty. He is said to have carried a ladle throughout the long years of his disciplinary Zen peregrinations. His idea was to serve in one of the most despised and most difficult positions in the monastery life—that is, as cook—and the ladle was his symbol. When he finally succeeded Tokusan (Teh-shan) as Zen master a monk approached him and asked: "What is that you have attained under Tokusan? How serene and self-contained you are!" "Empty-handed I went away from home, and empty-handed I returned." Is not this a practical explanation of the doctrine of "no abiding place"? The monks wanted their master Hyakujo (Pai-chang) to give a lecture on Zen. He said, "You attend to the farming and later on I will tell you all about Zen." After they had finished the work the master was requested to fulfil his promise, whereupon he opened out both his arms, but said not a word. This was his great sermon.

VII

SATORI, *OR ACQUIRING A NEW VIEWPOINT*[1]

THE object of Zen discipline consists in acquiring a new viewpoint for looking into the essence of things. If you have been in the habit of thinking logically according to the rules of dualism, rid yourself of it and you may come around somewhat to the viewpoint of Zen. You and I are supposedly living in the same world, but who can tell that the thing we popularly call a stone that is lying before my window is the same to both of us? You and I sip a cup of tea. That act is apparently alike to us both, but who can tell what a wide gap there is subjectively between your drinking and my drinking? In your drinking there may be no Zen, while mine is brim-full of it. The reason for it is: you move in a logical circle and I am out of it. Though there is in fact nothing new in the so-called new viewpoint of Zen, the term "new" is convenient to express the Zen way of viewing the world, but its use here is a condescension on the part of Zen.

This acquiring of a new viewpoint in Zen is called *satori* (*wu* in C.) and its verb form is *satoru*. Without it there is no Zen, for the life of Zen begins with the "opening of *satori*". *Satori* may be defined as intuitive looking-into, in contradistinction to intellectual and logical understanding. Whatever the definition, *satori* means the unfolding of a new world hitherto unperceived in the confusion of a dualistic mind. With this preliminary remark I wish the reader to ponder the following *mondo* (literally, "asking and answering"), which I hope will illustrate my statement.

A young monk asked Joshu to be instructed in the faith of Zen. Said the master:

"Have you had your breakfast, or not?"

"Yes, master, I have," answered the monk.

---

[1] This subject is more fully treated in my *Zen Essays*, I, pp. 215-50, and also in II, pp. 4 ff.

"Go and get your bowls washed," was the immediate response. And this suggestion at once opened the monk's mind to the truth of Zen.

Later on Ummon commented on the response, saying: "Was there any special instruction in this remark by Joshu, or was there not? If there was, what was it? If there was not, what *satori* was it which the monk attained?" Still later Suigan had the following retort on Ummon: "The great master Ummon does not know what is what; hence this comment of his. It is altogether unnecessary; it is like painting legs to a snake, or painting a beard to the eunuch. My view differs from his. That monk who seems to have attained a sort of *satori* goes to hell as straight as an arrow!"

What does all this mean—Joshu's remark about washing the bowls, the monk's attainment of *satori*, Ummon's alternatives, and Suigan's assurance? Are they speaking against one another, or is it much ado about nothing? To my mind, they are all pointing one way and the monk may go anywhere, but his *satori* is not to no purpose.

Tokusan was a great scholar of the *Diamond Sutra*. Learning that there was such a thing as Zen, ignoring all the written scriptures and directly laying hands on one's soul, he went to Ryutan to be instructed in the teaching. One day Tokusan was sitting outside trying to look into the mystery of Zen. Ryutan said, "Why don't you come in?" Replied Tokusan, "It is pitch dark." A candle was lighted and held out to Tokusan. When he was at the point of taking it Ryutan suddenly blew out the light, whereupon the mind of Tokusan was opened.

Hyakujo (Pai-chang) went out one day attending his master Baso (Ma-tsu), when they saw a flock of wild geese flying. Baso asked:

"What are they?"

"They are wild geese, sir."

"Whither are they flying?"

"They have flown away."

Baso, abruptly taking hold of Hyakujo's nose, gave it a twist. Overcome with pain, Hyakujo cried out: "Oh! Oh!"

Said Baso, "You say they have flown away, but all the same they have been here from the very first."

This made Hyakujo's back wet with perspiration; he had *satori*.

Is there any possible connection between the washing of the bowls and the blowing out of the candle and the twisting of the nose? We must say with Ummon: If there is none, how could they have all come to a realization of the truth of Zen? If there is, what is the inner relationship? What is this *satori*? What new point of view of looking at things is this?

Under Daiye (Ta-hui),[1] the great Zen master of the Sung dynasty, there was a monk named Doken (Tao-ch'ien), who had spent many years in the study of Zen, but who had not as yet uncovered its secrets, if there were any. He was quite discouraged when he was sent on an errand to a distant city. A trip requiring half a year to finish would be a hindrance rather than a help to his study. Sogen (Tsung-yuan), one of his fellow-students, was most sympathetic and said, "I will accompany you on this trip and do all I can for you; there is no reason why you cannot go on with your meditation even while travelling." One evening Doken despairingly implored his friend to assist him in the solution of the mystery of life. The friend said, "I am willing to help you in every way I can, but there are some things in which I cannot be of any help to you; these you must look after for yourself." Doken expressed the desire to know what these things were. Said his friend: "For instance, when you are hungry or thirsty, my eating of food or drinking will not fill your stomach; you must eat and drink for yourself. When you want to respond to the calls of nature you must take care of yourself, for I cannot be of any use to you. And then it will be nobody else but yourself that will carry your body along this highway." This friendly counsel at once opened the mind of the truth-seeking monk, who was so transported with his discovery that he did not know how to express his joy. Sogen said that his work was now done and that his further companionship would have no meaning after this; so he left Doken to continue his journey all by himself. After a half year Doken returned to his own monastery. Daiye, on his way down the mountains, happened to meet Doken and at once made the following remark, "This time he knows it all." What was it, let me ask, that flashed

[1] 1089-1163. A disciple of Yengo. See p. 116.

through Doken's mind when his friend Sogen gave him such matter-of-fact advice?

Kyogen (Hsiang-yen) was a disciple of Hyakujo (Pai-chang). After his master's death Kyogen went to Yisan (Kuei-shan), who had been a senior disciple of Hyakujo. Yisan asked him: "I am told that you have been studying under my late master, and also that you have remarkable intelligence. The understanding of Zen through this medium necessarily ends in intellectual analytical comprehension, which is not of much use; but nevertheless you may have had an insight into the truth of Zen. Let me have your view as to the reason of birth and death; that is, as to your own being before your parents had given birth to you."

Thus asked, Kyogen did not know how to reply. He retired into his own room and assiduously made research into the notes which he had taken of the sermons given by their late master. He failed to come across a suitable passage which he might present as his own view. He returned to Yisan and implored him to teach him in the faith of Zen, but Yisan replied: "I really have nothing to impart to you, and if I tried to do so you might have occasion to make me an object of ridicule. Besides, whatever I can tell you is my own and can never be yours." Kyogen was disappointed and considered him unkind. Finally he came to the decision to burn up all his notes and memoranda, which seemed to be of no help to his spiritual welfare, and, retiring altogether from the world, to spend the rest of his life in solitude and the simple life in accordance with Buddhist rules. He reasoned: "What is the use of studying Buddhism, which is so difficult to comprehend and which is too subtle to receive as instruction from another? I will be a plain homeless monk, troubled with no desire to master things too deep for thought." He left Yisan and built a hut near the tomb of Chu, the National Master at Nan-yang. One day he was weeding and sweeping the ground when a pebble which he had swept away struck a bamboo; the unexpected sound produced by the percussion elevated his mind to a state of *satori*. His joy was boundless. The question proposed by Yisan became transparent; he felt as if meeting his lost parents. Besides, he came to realize the kindness of Yisan in refusing him instruction, for now he realized that this experience could not have happened to him if Yisan had been unkind enough to explain things to him.

Cannot Zen be so explained that a master can lead all his pupils to enlightenment through explanation? Is *satori* something that is not at all capable of intellectual analysis? Yes, it is an experience which no amount of explanation or argument can make communicable to others unless the latter themselves had it previously. If *satori* is amenable to analysis in the sense that by so doing it becomes perfectly clear to another who has never had it, that *satori* will be no *satori*. For a *satori* turned into a concept ceases to be itself; and there will no more be a Zen experience. Therefore, all that we can do in Zen in the way of instruction is to indicate, or to suggest, or to show the way so that one's attention may be directed towards the goal. As to attaining the goal and taking hold of the thing itself, this must be done by one's own hands, for nobody else can do it for one. As regards the indication, it lies everywhere. When a man's mind is matured for *satori* it tumbles over one everywhere. An inarticulate sound, an unintelligent remark, a blooming flower, or a trivial incident such as stumbling, is the condition or occasion that will open his mind to *satori*. Apparently, an insignificant event produces an effect which in importance is altogether out of proportion. The light touch of an igniting wire, and an explosion follows which will shake the very foundation of the earth. All the causes, all the conditions of *satori* are in the mind; they are merely waiting for the maturing. When the mind is ready for some reasons or others, a bird flies, or a bell rings, and you at once return to your original home; that is, you discover your now real self. From the very beginning nothing has been kept from you, all that you wished to see has been there all the time before you, it was only yourself that closed the eye to the fact. Therefore, there is in Zen nothing to explain, nothing to teach, that will add to your knowledge. Unless it grows out of yourself no knowledge is really yours, it is only a borrowed plumage.

Kozankoku (Huang Shan-ku), a Confucian poet and statesman of the Sung, came to Kwaido (Hui-t'ang) to be initiated into Zen. Said the Zen master: "There is a passage in the text with which you are perfectly familiar which fitly describes the teaching of Zen. Did not Confucius declare: 'Do you think I am hiding things from you, O my disciples? Indeed, I have nothing to hide from you.'" Kozankoku tried to answer, but Kwaido immediately checked him by saying, "No, no!" The Confucian scholar felt troubled in mind but did not know how to express himself. Some time later they were having a walk in the mountains; the wild laurel was in full bloom and the air was redolent with its scent. Asked the Zen master, "Do you smell it?" When the Confucian answered affirmatively, Kwaido said, "There, I have nothing to hide from you." This reminder at once led Kozankoku's mind to the opening of a *satori*.

These examples will suffice to show what *satori* is and how it unfolds itself. The reader may ask, however: "After the perusal of all your explanations or indications, we are not a whit wiser. Can you not definitely describe the content of *satori*, if there is any? Your examples and statements are tentative enough, but we simply know how the wind blows; where is the port the boat finally makes for?" To this the Zen devotee may answer: As far as content goes, there is none in either *satori* or Zen that can be described or presented or demonstrated for your intellectual appreciation. For Zen has no business with ideas, and *satori* is a sort of inner perception—not the perception, indeed, of a single individual object but the perception of Reality itself, so to speak. The ultimate destination of *satori* is towards the Self; it has no other end but to be back within oneself. Therefore, said Joshu, "Have a cup of tea." Therefore, said Nansen, "This is such a good sickle, it cuts so well." This is the way the Self functions, and it must be caught, if at all catchable, in the midst of its functioning.

As *satori* strikes at the primary root of existence, its attainment generally marks a turning point in one's life. The attainment, however, must be thoroughgoing and clear-cut; a lukewarm *satori*, if there is such a thing, is worse than no *satori*. See the following examples:

When Rinzai (Lin-chi) was meekly submitting to the thirty blows of Obaku (Huang-po), he presented a pitiable sight, but as soon as he had attained *satori* he was quite a different personage. His first exclamation was, "There is not much after all in the Buddhism of Obaku." And when he again saw the reproachful Obaku, he returned his favour by giving him a slap in the face. "What arrogance! What impudence!" one may think. But there was reason in Rinzai's rudeness; no wonder Obaku was quite pleased with this treatment.

When Tokusan (Te-shan) gained an insight into the truth of Zen he immediately took out all his commentaries on the *Diamond Sutra*, once so valued and considered indispensable that he had to carry them wherever he went, and set fire to them, reducing all the manuscripts to ashes. He exclaimed, "However deep one's knowledge of abstruse philosophy, it is like a piece of hair flying in the vastness of space; however important one's experience in things worldly, it is like a drop of water thrown into an unfathomable abyss."

One day, following the incident of the flying geese, to which reference was made elsewhere, Baso appeared in the preaching hall and was about to speak before a congregation, when Hyakujo, whose nose was literally put out of joint, came forward and began to roll up the matting which is spread before the Buddha for the master to kneel. The rolling up generally means the end of the sermon. Baso, without protesting, came down from the pulpit and returned to his room. He sent for Hyakujo and asked him why he rolled up the matting before he had even uttered a word. Replied Hyakujo, "Yesterday you twisted my nose and it was quite painful." Said Baso, "Where were your thoughts wandering?" Hyakujo replied, "Today it is no longer painful." With this Baso admitted Hyakujo's understanding.

These examples are sufficient to show what changes are produced in one's mind by the attainment of *satori*. Before *satori*, how helpless those monks were! They were like travellers lost in the desert. But after *satori* they behave like absolute monarchs; they are no longer slaves to anybody, they are themselves master.

After these remarks the following points about the opening of the mind that is called *satori* may be observed and summarized.

94

1. People often imagine that the discipline of Zen is to produce a state of self-suggestion through meditation. This entirely misses the mark, as can be seen from the various instances cited above. *Satori* does not consist in producing a certain premeditated condition by intensely thinking of it. It is acquiring a new point of view for looking at things. Ever since the unfoldment of consciousness we have been led to respond to the inner and outer conditions in a certain conceptual and analytical manner. The discipline of Zen consists in upsetting this groundwork once for all and reconstructing the old frame on an entirely new basis. It is evident, therefore, that meditating on metaphysical and symbolical statements, which are products of a relative consciousness, play no part in Zen.

2. Without the attainment of *satori* no one can enter into the truth of Zen. *Satori* is the sudden flashing into consciousness of a new truth hitherto undreamed of. It is a sort of mental catastrophe taking place all at once, after much piling up of matters intellectual and demonstrative. The piling has reached a limit of stability and the whole edifice has come tumbling to the ground, when, behold, a new heaven is open to full survey. When the freezing point is reached, water suddenly turns into ice; the liquid has suddenly turned into a solid body and no more flows freely. *Satori* comes upon a man unawares, when he feels that he has exhausted his whole being. Religiously, it is a new birth; intellectually, it is the acquiring of a new viewpoint. The world now appears as if dressed in a new garment, which seems to cover up all the unsightliness of dualism, which is called delusion in Buddhist phraseology.

3. *Satori* is the *raison d'être* of Zen without which Zen is no Zen. Therefore every contrivance, disciplinary or doctrinal, is directed toward *satori*. Zen masters could not remain patient for *satori* to come by itself; that is, to come sporadically or at its own pleasure. In their earnestness to aid their disciples in the search after the truth of Zen their manifestly enigmatical presentations were designed to create in their disciples a state of mind which would more systematically open the way to enlightenment. All the intellectual demonstrations and exhortatory persuasions so far carried out by most religious and philosophical leaders

95

had failed to produce the desired effect, and their disciples thereby had been farther and farther led astray. Especially was this the case when Buddhism was first introduced into China, with all its Indian heritage of highly metaphysical abstractions and most complicated systems of Yoga discipline, which left the more practical Chinese at a loss as to how to grasp the central point of the doctrine of Sakyamuni. Bodhidharma, the Sixth Patriarch, Baso, and other Chinese masters noticed this fact, and the proclamation and development of Zen was the natural outcome. By them *satori* was placed above sutra-learning and scholarly discussions of the sastras and was identified with Zen itself. Zen, therefore, without *satori* is like pepper without its pungency. But there is also such a thing as too much attachment to the experience of *satori*, which is to be detested.

4. This emphasizing of *satori* in Zen makes the fact quite significant that Zen is not a system of Dhyana as practised in India and by other Buddhist schools in China. By Dhyana is generally understood a kind of meditation or contemplation directed toward some fixed thought; in Hinayana Buddhism it was the thought of transiency, while in the Mahayana it was more often the doctrine of emptiness. When the mind has been so trained as to be able to realize a state of perfect void in which there is not a trace of consciousness left, even the sense of being unconscious having departed; in other words, when all forms of mental activity are swept away clean from the field of consciousness, leaving the mind like the sky devoid of every speck of cloud, a mere broad expanse of blue, Dhyana is said to have reached its perfection. This may be called ecstasy or trance, but it is not Zen. In Zen there must be *satori*; there must be a general mental upheaval which destroys the old accumulations of intellection and lays down the foundation for a new life; there must be the awakening of a new sense which will review the old things from a hitherto undreamed-of angle of observation. In Dhyana there are none of these things, for it is merely a quieting exercise of mind. As such Dhyana doubtless has its own merit, but Zen must not be identified with it.

5. *Satori* is not seeing God as he is, as might be contended

by some Christian mystics. Zen has from the beginning made clear and insisted upon the main thesis, which is to see into the work of creation; the creator may be found busy moulding his universe, or he may be absent from his workshop, but Zen goes on with its own work. It is not dependent upon the support of a creator; when it grasps the reason for living a life, it is satisfied. Hoyen (Fa-yen, died 1104) of Go-so-san used to produce his own hand and ask his disciples why it was called a hand. When we know the reason, there is *satori* and we have Zen. Whereas with the God of mysticism there is the grasping of a definite object; when you have God, what is no-God is excluded. This is self-limiting. Zen wants absolute freedom, even from God. "No abiding place" means that very thing; "Cleanse your mouth when you utter the word Buddha" amounts to the same thing. It is not that Zen wants to be morbidly unholy and godless, but that it recognizes the incompleteness of a mere name. Therefore, when Yakusan (Yueh-shan, 751–834) was asked to give a lecture, he did not say a word, but instead came down from the pulpit and went off to his own room. Hyakujo merely walked forward a few steps, stood still, and then opened out his arms, which was his exposition of the great principle.

6. *Satori* is not a morbid state of mind, a fit subject for the study of abnormal psychology. If anything, it is a perfectly normal state of mind. When I speak of a mental upheaval, some may be led to consider Zen as something to be shunned by ordinary people. This is a most mistaken view of Zen, but one unfortunately often held by prejudiced critics. As Joshu declared, "Zen is your everyday thought"; it all depends on the adjustment of the hinge whether the door opens in or opens out. Even in the twinkling of an eye the whole affair is changed and you have Zen, and you are as perfect and as normal as ever. More than that, you have acquired in the meantime something altogether new. All your mental activities will now be working to a different key, which will be more satisfying, more peaceful, and fuller of joy than anything you ever experienced before The tone of life will be altered. There is something rejuvenating in the possession of Zen. The spring flowers look prettier, and the mountain stream runs cooler and more trans-

parent. The subjective revolution that brings about this state of things cannot be called abnormal. When life becomes more enjoyable and its expanse broadens to include the universe itself, there must be something in *satori* that is quite precious and well worth one's striving after.

VIII

THE KOAN[1]

ZEN is a unique product of the Oriental mind and its uniqueness consists, so far as its practical aspect goes, in its methodical training of the mind in order to mature it to the state of *satori*, when all its secrets are revealed. Zen may be called a form of mysticism, but it differs from all other forms of it in system, in discipline, and in final attainment. By this I mean principally the *koan* exercise and *zazen*.

Zazen, or its Sanskrit equivalent *dhyana*, means sitting cross-legged in quietude and in deep contemplation. The practice originated in India and spread all over the East. It has been going on through centuries now, and the modern followers of Zen still strictly observe it. In this respect *zazen* is the prevailing practical method of spiritual discipline in the East, but when it is used in connection with the *koan* it assumes a special feature and becomes the monopoly of Zen.

To explain fully what *zazen* or Dhyana is is not the object of this chapter, which is chiefly concerned with the *koan* as the most essential feature of Zen now practised in the Far East. Originally in Buddhism, Dhyana was one of its three branches of discipline: *Sila* (moral precepts), *Dhyana* (contemplation), and *Prajna* (wisdom). Good Buddhists are supposed to be morally observant of all the precepts laid down by the Buddha, to be thoroughly versed in the methods for keeping their inordinate passions well under control, and finally to be intellectual[2] enough to know all the intricacies of logic in the advancement of Buddhist metaphysics. When a man lacks in any of these qualifications he cannot be said to be a very good follower of Sakyamuni. But as time went on differentiation took place, and some Buddhists came to emphasize one of the three more strongly than the

---

[1] For a fuller treatment of the subject, see my *Zen Essays*, II.

[2] *Prajna* is the highest power of intuition which sounds the depths of our soul-life, and is naturally much more than merely intellectual. For further information read a chapter on the Prajnaparamita in my *Zen Essays*, III.

others. Some were moralists more than anything else, others were students of Dhyana, and still others were devoted to the mastery of intellectual subtleties implied in the teachings of Buddhism. Zen followers may be considered practisers of Dhyana, but in Zen Dhyana has ceased to be understood in its primitive sense; for Zen has now its own object in the practice of this particular Indian form of spiritual exercises.

According to the *Mahayana Sastra* quoted in the *Dhyana-Paramita Systematically Expounded* by Chi-sha Daishi, the founder of the T'ien-tai sect, Dhyana is practised in order to fulfil the four great vows[1] cherished by every pious Buddhist:

> Dhyana is the storage of good wisdom,
> And the farm of blissful merits;
> Like unto water free from impurities,
> Dhyana washes all the dust of passion;
> Dhyana is the armour wrought of vajra,
> Which shields the wearer from the arrows of
>   evil desires;
> Though you may not yet have attained to a
>   state of non-doing,
> You are already gaining towards Nirvana;
> For you will gain the Vajra-samadhi,
> You will break in pieces the Hindrances and
>   Restrictions, though mountain-high they are,
> You will attain the Six Miraculous Powers,
> And you will be able to deliver numberless
>   beings;
> When the dust of Annoyance rises so high as
>   to screen the heavenly sun,
> Great showers may wash it away,
> The wind of Intellectual Enlightenment may
>   remove it,
> But it is Dhyana that will destroy it altogether.

Dhyana comes from the root *dhi*, meaning "to perceive", "to reflect upon", "to fix the mind upon"; while *dhi* etymologically may have some connection with *dha*, "to hold", "to keep",

---

[1] 1. All sentient beings, however infinite, I vow to save. 2. All the passions, however inexhaustible, I vow to cut asunder. 3. All the holy teachings, however innumerable, I vow to learn. 4. All the Buddha-ways, however unsurpassable, I vow to fulfil.

"to maintain". Dhyana thus means to hold one's thought collected, not to let thought wander away from its legitimate path; that is, it means to have the mind concentrated on a single subject of thought. Therefore, when Zen or Dhyana is practised, all the outer details are to be so controlled as to bring the mind into the most favourable condition in which it will gradually rise above the turbulence of passions and sensualities. For instance, eating and drinking have to be properly regulated; sleep is not to be too much indulged in; the body is to be kept in an easy and comfortable position, but straight and erect; and as to the control of breathing, the Indians are, as is well known, consummate artists. Next, the choice of the place where the Dhyana-practiser is to sit is another important consideration, and naturally such places as the market, the factory, or the business office may better be avoided. There are many more rules or suggestions relating to the control of the body and the mind, which are fully treated in Chi-sha's work on *Dhyana-Paramita*.[1]

As is evident even from this brief account of Dhyana, *zazen* as is practised by Zen devotees has not the same object in mind as is the case with Buddhists generally. In Zen, Dhyana or *zazen* is used as the means of reaching the solution of the *koan*. Zen does not make Dhyana an end in itself, for apart from the *koan* exercise, the practising of *zazen* is a secondary consideration. It is no doubt a necessary accompaniment to the mastery of Zen; even when the *koan* is understood, its deep spiritual truth will not be driven home to the mind of the Zen student if he is not thoroughly trained in *zazen*. *Koan* and *zazen* are the two handmaids of Zen; the first is the eye and the second is the foot.

In the early days of Buddhism in China, philosophical discussion first attracted the attention of the earnest students of Buddhism and such sutras as the *Avatamsaka, Pundarika, Prajna-paramita, Nirvana*, etc., were early translated into Chinese. The deep metaphysical thoughts contained in these sacred texts interested Chinese scholars more than did other matters that were also to be found in them, and it was probably chiefly due to the incomparable Kumarajiva that a great impetus was given

---

[1] As regards the practice of *zazen* in Japan, see my *Zen Essays*, II, pp. 284-7.

to the Chinese Buddhists to the intellectual mastery of the texts. The ethical study of Buddhism came next. When Bodhidharma, the First Patriarch of Zen, came to China in the sixth century, he was looked upon somewhat askance as a sort of heretic. Scholars of Buddhist philosophy did not understand him and disliked him. Even when Yeno (Hui-neng), the Sixth Patriarch, came out of obscurity and self-concealment to announce himself as the rightful transmitter of Zen, he was not very much noticed by the other practisers of Dhyana. So far Dhyana or *zazen* had been practised chiefly after the Hinayana fashion, as we read in the biographical writings of earlier Buddhism in China, and also as we can infer from the sutras on Dhyana which were translated down to those days. It was a generation or two after Yeno that Zen, as we understand it now, really came into existence, which thereafter rapidly developed so as to overshadow all the other Buddhist schools. At present there are no Buddhist monasteries in China which do not belong to the Zen sect, and most of them are of the Rinzai school of Zen.[1] One reason among others for this conquest is to be found in the practice of *zazen* as the means of mastering the *koan* and thus attaining *satori*.

Ko-an literally means "a public document" or "authoritative statute"—a term coming into vogue toward the end of the T'ang dynasty. It now denotes some anecdote of an ancient master, or a dialogue between a master and monks, or a statement or question put forward by a teacher, all of which are used as the means for opening one's mind to the truth of Zen. In the beginning, of course, there was no *koan* as we understand it now; it is a kind of artificial instrument devised out of the fullness of heart by later Zen masters, who by this means would force the evolution of Zen consciousness in the minds of their less endowed disciples.

The mind may grow by itself even when it is left to nature to achieve her own ends, but man cannot always wait for her, he likes to meddle for better or worse. He is never patient; whenever there is a chance to put his fingers in, he is sure to do so.

[1] At present Chinese Buddhism is a strange mixture of Zen and Nembutsu, though most monasteries profess to belong to the Zen sect. They recite the *Amitabha sutra* along with the *Prajnahridaya*.

The interference is sometimes helpful, sometimes decidedly not. As a rule it works two ways. We welcome human interference when more is to be gained than lost and call it improvement and progress; but when it turns out otherwise we call it retrogression. Civilization is human and artificial; some are not satisfied with it and want to go back to nature. Well, so-called modern progress is by no means unmitigated bliss, but on the whole, at least on the material side of life, we seem to be better off these days than ever before, and we see some signs of further improvement. Therefore, our grumblings generally are not very vehemently asserted.

In a similar way, the introduction of the system of *koan* into Zen, pure, natural, and elementary, is at once a deterioration and an improvement. But once brought out into existence, the system seems very hard to do away with. It was, of course, quite human on the part of the Zen master to be thinking of his less fortunate brothers whose natural endowments were not so rich as his own, and who, therefore, would be likely to miss opportunities to come into the truth of Zen. He wanted to impart to them, if possible, the same wonderful bliss of the understanding which he had gained through the mastery of Zen. His motherly instinct made him think of some way to open or even to coerce the minds of his disciples to the unknown beauties of *satori*, which, when left to their own ignorant ways, would never come upon them except by a happy rare chance. The master knew that the device of a *koan* was an artificiality and a superfluity; for unless Zen grew out of a man's own inner activity it could not be truly genuine and full of creative vitality as it ought to be. But even a semblance would be a blessing when the genuine thing is so difficult and rare to have; and, moreover, it was likely, if it is left to itself, to disappear altogether out of the lore of human experience. The semblance is not necessarily a mere makeshift but may have in it something quite true and full of possibilities; for the system of *koan* and *zazen*, when properly made use of, really does unfold the mind to the truth of Zen. Why then should we not adopt it and work it out to its fullness?

At the beginning, a Zen master was a kind of self-made man; he had no school education, he had not been sent to college to pass through a certain course of studies, but out of an inner impelling necessity which stirred up his spirit he could not help going about and picking up whatever knowledge he needed. He was perfected by himself. Of course, he had a teacher, but the teacher did not help him in the way scholars nowadays are helped—helped too frequently, indeed, beyond the actual needs of the disciple, more than is really good for him. This lack of soft education made the ancient Zen master all the stronger and more full of virility. This was the reason why, in those early days of Zen—that is, during the T'ang dynasty—it was so active, so brilliant, so intense. When the *koan* system came into vogue during the Sung dynasty the halcyon days of Zen were almost over and it gradually showed signs of decline and senility.

Here then is one of the first *koans* given to latter-day students. When the Sixth Patriarch was asked by the monk Myo (Ming) what Zen was, he said: "When your mind is not dwelling on the dualism of good and evil, what is your original face before you were born?" (Show me this "face" and you get into the mystery of Zen. Who are you before Abraham was born? When you have had a personal, intimate interview with this personage, you will better know who you are and who God is. The monk is here told to shake hands with this original man, or, if metaphysically put, with his own inner self.)

When this question was put to the monk Myo, he was already mentally ready to see into the truth of it. The questioning is merely on the surface, it is really an affirmation meant to open the mind of the listener. The Patriarch noticed that Myo's mind was on the verge of unfolding itself to the truth of Zen. The monk had been groping in the dark long and earnestly; his mind had become mature, so mature indeed that it was like a ripe fruit which required only a slight shaking to cause it to drop on the ground; his mind required only a final touch by the hand of the master. The demand for "the original face" was the last finish necessary, and Myo's mind instantly opened and grasped the truth. But when this statement in the form of a question about "the original face" is given to a novice, who has had no previous discipline in Zen as Myo had, it is usually given with the intention to awaken the student's mind to the fact that what he has so far accepted as a commonplace fact, or as a logical impossibility, is not necessarily so, and that his former way of looking at things was not always correct or helpful to his spiritual welfare. After this is realized, the student might dwell on the statement itself and endeavour to get at its truth if it has any. To force the student to assume this inquiring attitude is the aim of the *koan*. The student must then go on with his inquiring attitude until he comes to the edge of a mental precipice, as it were, where there are no other alternatives but to leap over. This giving up of his last hold on life will bring the student to a full view of "his original face", as desired by the statement of the Sixth Patriarch. Thus it can be seen that the *koan* is not handled now in precisely the same way that it was in those earlier days. As first proposed, it was the culmination, so to speak, of all that had been working in the mind of the monk Myo, whose elaboration herein received its final finish; instead of coming at the beginning of the Zen exercise, as it does now, the Sixth Patriarch's question came at the end of the race. But in modern days the *koan* is used as a starter; it gives an initial movement to the racing for Zen experience. More or less mechanical in the beginning, the movement acquires the tone needed for the maturing of Zen consciousness; the *koan* works as a leaven. When the sufficient conditions obtain, the mind unfolds itself into the full bloom of a *satori*. To use a *koan* thus instrumentally for the opening of the mind to its own secrets is characteristic of modern Zen.

Hakuin used to produce one of his hands and demand of his disciples to hear the sound of it. Ordinarily a sound is heard only when two hands are clapped, and in that sense no possible sound can come from one hand alone. Hakuin wants, however, to strike at the root of our everyday experience, which is constructed on a so-called scientific or logical basis. This fundamental overthrowing is necessary in order to build up a new order of things on the basis of Zen experience. Hence this apparently most unnatural and therefore illogical demand made by Hakuin on his pupils. The former *koan* was about "the face", something to look at, while the latter is about "the sound", something that appeals to the sense of hearing; but the ultimate purport of both is the same; both are meant to open up

105

the secret chamber of the mind, where the devotees can find numberless treasures stored. The sense of seeing or hearing has nothing to do with the essential meaning of the *koan*; as the Zen masters say, the *koan* is only a piece of brick used to knock at the gate, an index-finger pointing at the moon. It is only intended to synthesize or transcend—whichever expression you may choose—the dualism of the senses. So long as the mind is not free to perceive a sound produced by one hand, it is limited and is divided against itself. Instead of grasping the key to the secrets of creation, the mind is hopelessly buried in the relativity of things, and, therefore, in their superficiality. Until the mind is free from the fetters, the time never comes for it to view the whole world with any amount of satisfaction. The sound of one hand as a matter of fact reaches the highest heaven as well as the lowest hell, just as one's original face looks over the entire field of creation even to the end of time. Hakuin and the Sixth Patriarch stand on the same platform with their hands mutually joined.

To mention another instance. When Joshu was asked about the significance of Bodhidharma's coming east (which, proverbially, is the same as asking about the fundamental principle of Buddhism), he replied, "The cypress-tree in the courtyard."

"You are talking," said the monk, "of an objective symbol."

"No, I am not talking of an objective symbol."

"Then," asked the monk again, "what is the ultimate principle of Buddhism?"

"The cypress-tree in the courtyard," again replied Joshu.

This is also given to a beginner as a *koan*.

Abstractly speaking, these *koans* cannot be said to be altogether nonsensical even from a common-sense point of view, and if we want to reason about them there is perhaps room enough to do so. For instance, some may regard Hakuin's one hand as symbolizing the universe or the unconditioned, and Joshu's cypress-tree as a concrete manifestation of the highest principle, through which the pantheistic tendency of Buddhism may be recognized. But to understand the *koan* thus intellectually is not Zen, nor is such metaphysical symbolism at all present here. Under no circumstances ought Zen to be confounded with philosophy; Zen has its own reason for standing for itself, and this fact must never be lost sight of; otherwise, the entire structure of Zen falls to pieces. The "cypress-tree" is forever a cypress-tree and has nothing to do with pantheism or any other "ism". Joshu was not a philosopher even in its broadest and most popular sense; he was a Zen master through and through, and all that comes forth from his lips is an utterance directly ensuing from his spiritual experience. Therefore, apart from this much of "subjectivism", though really there are no such dualities in Zen as subject and object, thought and the world, the "cypress-tree" utterly loses its significance. If it is an intellectual or conceptual statement, we may endeavour to understand its meaning through the ratiocinative chain of ideas as contained in it, and we may come to imagine that we have finally solved the difficulty; but Zen masters will assure you that even then Zen is yet three thousand miles away from you, and the spirit of Joshu will be heard laughing at you from behind the screen, which after all you had failed to remove. The *koan* is intended to be nourished in those recesses of the mind where no logical analysis can ever reach. When the mind matures so that it becomes attuned to a similar frame to that of Joshu, the meaning of the "cypress-tree" will reveal itself, and without further questioning you will be convinced that you now know it all.

A disciple of Joshu called Kaku-tetsu-shi (Chueh T'ieh-tzu) was asked after the death of his master whether he had really made the statement about the cypress-tree in response to the question, "What is the fundamental principle of Buddhism?" The disciple unhesitatingly declared, "My master never made that statement." This was a direct contradiction of the fact, for everybody then knew that Joshu had made it, and the one who asked Kaku-tetsu-shi about it was himself not ignorant of it. His questioning was to see what insight this disciple of Joshu had into the meaning of the story of the cypress-tree. Therefore, the questioner further pursued Tetsu by saying, "But this is asserted by everybody, and how can you deny it?" Tetsu insisted, "My master never said it; and you will do well if you do not thus disparage him." What an audacious statement! But those that know Zen know that this flat denial is the irrevocable proof that Tetsu thoroughly understood the spirit of his master. His

107

Zen was beyond question. But from our common-sense point of view no amount of intellectual resourcefulness can be brought upon his flat denial so that it can somehow be reconciled with the plain fact itself. Zen is, therefore, quite merciless toward those critics who take the story of the cypress-tree for an expression savouring of Mahayana pantheism.

The *koans*, therefore, as we have seen, are generally such as to shut up all possible avenues to rationalization. After a few presentations of your views in the interview with the master, which is technically called *san-zen*, you are sure to come to the end of your resources, and this coming to a *cul-de-sac* is really the true starting point in the study of Zen. No one can enter into Zen without this experience. When this point is reached the *koans* may be regarded as having accomplished a half of the object for which they stand.

To speak conventionally—and I think it is easier for the general reader to see Zen thus presented—there are unknown recesses in our minds which lie beyond the threshold of the relatively constructed consciousness. To designate them as "sub-consciousness" or "supra-consciousness" is not correct. The word "beyond" is used simply because it is a most convenient term to indicate their whereabouts. But as a matter of fact there is no "beyond", no "underneath", no "upon" in our consciousness. The mind is one indivisible whole and cannot be torn in pieces. The so-called *terra incognita* is the concession of Zen to our ordinary way of talking, because whatever field of consciousness that is known to us is generally filled with conceptual riffraff, and to get rid of them, which is absolutely necessary for maturing Zen experience, the Zen psychologist sometimes points to the presence of some inaccessible region in our minds. Though in actuality there is no such region apart from our everyday consciousness, we talk of it as generally more easily comprehensible by us. When the *koan* breaks down all the hindrances to the ultimate truth, we all realize that there are, after all, no such things as "hidden recesses of mind" or even the truth of Zen appearing all the time so mysterious.

The *koan* is neither a riddle nor a witty remark. It has a most definite objective, the arousing of doubt and pushing it to its furthest limits. A statement built upon a logical basis is approachable through its rationality; whatever doubt or difficulty we may have had about it dissolves itself by pursuing the natural current of ideas. All rivers are sure to pour into the ocean; but the *koan* is an iron wall standing in the way and threatening to overcome one's every intellectual effort to pass. When Joshu says "the cypress-tree in the courtyard", or when Hakuin puts out his one hand, there is no logical way to get around it. You feel as if your march of thought had been suddenly cut short. You hesitate, you doubt, you are troubled and agitated, not knowing how to break through the wall which seems altogether impassable. When this climax is reached, your whole personality, your inmost will, your deepest nature, determined to bring the situation to an issue, throws itself with no thought of self or no-self, of this or that, directly and unreservedly against the iron wall of the *koan*. This throwing your entire being against the *koan* unexpectedly opens up a hitherto unknown region of the mind. Intellectually, this is the transcending of the limits of logical dualism, but at the same time it is a regeneration, the awakening of an inner sense which enables one to look into the actual working of things. For the first time the meaning of the *koan* becomes clear, and in the same way that one knows that ice is cold and freezing. The eye sees, the ear hears, to be sure, but it is the mind as a whole that has *satori*; it is an act of perception, no doubt, but it is a perception of the highest order. Here lies the value of the Zen discipline, as it gives birth to the unshakable conviction that there is something indeed going beyond mere intellection.

The wall of *koan* once broken through and the intellectual obstructions well cleared off, you come back, so to speak, to your everyday relatively constructed consciousness. The one hand does not give out a sound until it is clapped by the other. The cypress-tree stands straight before the window; all human beings have the nose vertically set and the eyes horizontally arranged. Zen is now the most ordinary thing in the world. A field that we formerly supposed to lie far beyond is now found to be the very field in which we walk, day in, day out. When we come out of *satori* we see the familiar world with all its multitudinous objects and ideas together with their logicalness, and pronounce them "good".

When there was as yet no system of *koan*, Zen was more natural and purer perhaps, but it was only the few elect who could get into the spirit of it. Supposing you had lived in those days, what would you do if you were roughly shaken by the shoulder? How would you take it if you were called a dry dirt-scraper? Or if you were simply requested to hand the cushion over there, and, when you had handed it to the master, to be struck with it? If you had a determination to fathom the depths of Zen as strong as steel, and a faith in the "reasonableness" of Zen which was as firm as the earth, you, after many years of meditation, might succeed in mastering Zen; but such examples are rare in our modern days; we are so distracted with all kinds of business that we are unable to walk all by ourselves into the labyrinthine passageway of Zen. In the early days of the T'ang dynasty people were more simple-hearted and believing, their minds were not crammed with intellectual biases. But this state of affairs could not, in the nature of things, last very long; to maintain the vitality of Zen it was necessary to find some device whereby Zen could be made more approachable and to that extent more popular; the *koan* exercise had to be established for the benefit of the rising generations and also for the coming ones. Though it is in the being of Zen that it can never be a popular religion in the sense that Shin Buddhism or Christianity is, yet the fact that it has kept up its line of transmission unbroken for so many centuries is, in my view, principally due to the system of *koan*. In China, where Zen originated, it no longer exists in its pure form; the line of transmission is no more, so transfused is it with the Pure Land practice of invoking the Buddha-name. It is only in Japan that Zen is still virile and still finds its orthodox exponents; and there is every reason to believe that this is due to the system of reviewing the *koans* in connection with the practice of *zazen*. There is no doubt that this system is largely artificial and harbours grave pitfalls, but the life of Zen runs through it when it is properly handled. To those who pursue it judiciously under a really competent master, Zen-experience is possible and a state of *satori* will surely come.

Thus we can see that this Zen-experience is something realizable by going through a certain process of training. That is, the *koan* exercise is a system definitely set up with a definite object in view. Zen is not like other forms of mysticism, entirely left to the sporadic nature or capriciousness of luck for its experience. The systematization of *koan* is, therefore, the one thing that is most characteristic of Zen. It is this that saves Zen from sinking into trance, from becoming absorbed in mere contemplation, from turning into an exercise in tranquillization. Zen attempts to take hold of life in its act of living; to stop the flow of life and to look into it is not the business of Zen. The constant presence of the *koan* before our mental vision keeps the mind always occupied; that is, in full activity. *Satori* is attained in the midst of this activity and not by suppressing it, as some may imagine. How much Zen differs from "meditation" as the latter is generally understood, and practised, we now can see better from what has been said above as regards the nature of the *koan*.

The systematizing of Zen began as early as the Five Dynasties in China—that is, in the tenth century—but its completion was due to the genius of Hakuin (1683–1768) who lived in the Tokugawa era. Whatever one may say against the abuses of the *koan*, it was the *koan* that saved Japanese Zen from total annihilation. Consider how Chinese Zen is faring these days; so far as we can gather it is more or less a mere name; and again notice the general tendency shown in the practice of Zen by adherents of the Soto school in present-day Japan. We cannot deny that there are many good points in Soto, which ought to be carefully studied, but as to the living of Zen there is perhaps greater activity in the Rinzai, which employs the *koan* system.

One may say: "If Zen is really so far beyond the intellectual ken as you claim it to be, there ought not to be any system in it; in fact, there could not be any, for the very conception of a system is intellectual. To be thoroughly consistent, Zen should remain a simple absolute experience excluding all that savours of process or system or discipline. The *koan* must be an excrescence, a superfluity, indeed a contradiction." Theoretically, or rather from the absolute point of view, this is quite correct; therefore, when Zen is asserted "straightforwardly" it recognizes no *koan* and knows of no round-about way of proclaiming itself. Just a stick, a fan, or a word! Even when you say, "It is a stick," or "I hear a sound," or "I see the fist," Zen is no more there. It is like a flash of lightning, there is no room, no time, in Zen even for a thought to be conceived. We speak of a *koan* or a system only when we come to the practical or conventional side of it. As has been said before, it is really a condescension, an apology, a compromise, that this present work has been written; much more the whole systematization of Zen.

To outsiders this "systematization" appears to be no systematization, for it is full of contradictions, and even among the Zen masters themselves there is a great deal of discrepancy, which is quite disconcerting. What one asserts another flatly denies or makes a sarcastic remark about it, so that the uninitiated are at a loss what to make out of all these everlasting and hopeless entanglements. But the fact is that Zen really ought not to be considered from its surface; such terms as system, rationality, consistency, contradiction, or discordance belong to the surface of Zen; to understand Zen we are to turn up the whole piece of brocade and examine it from the other side, where we can trace at a glance all the intricacies of woof and warp. This reversing of the order is very much needed in Zen.

Let us quote an example to see how it is treated by different masters. Funyo, a great Zen master of the T'ang dynasty, said, "If a man knows what this staff is, his study of Zen comes to a close." This seems to be a simple enough *koan*. The master generally carries a long staff which is now a kind of insignia of his religious authority, but in ancient days it was really a travelling stick that was useful in climbing mountains or fording streams. Being one of the most familiar objects, it is produced any time by a master before his congregation to illustrate a sermon; it is often the subject of a great discussion among the monks. Cho of Rokutan, another Zen master, apparently opposed the view of the preceding master, Funyo, when he declared, "If a man knows what the staff is, he will go to hell as straight as an arrow flies." If this is the case, no one will be induced to study Zen; but what does Cho really mean? Ho-an, still another Zen master, makes a statement about this staff, which is not radical; he is quite rational and innocent when he says, "If a man knows what the staff is, let him take it and put it up against the wall over there." Are these masters all asserting the same fact and pointing to the same truth? Or are they not only in words but in fact and truth contradicting one another? Let us examine more masters concerning the staff.

Suiryu one day ascended the pulpit and bringing forth his staff made this confession: "My twenty years' residence in this monastery is due to the virtue of this."

A monk stepped forward and asked, "What virtue did you gain out of that?"

"Supporting myself with this, I cross the streams, I pass over the mountains; indeed, without it, what can I do?"

Later Shokei, another master, hearing of this remark, said, "If I were he, I would not say that."

"What would you say?" came quickly from the monk.

Shokei now took the staff, came down to the ground, and walked away.

Ho-an now makes the observation about these two masters: "Suiryu's staff was a pretty good one, but what a pity! it has a dragon's head with a snake's tail. It makes Shokei follow him up, and the result is another pity: his was like putting speckles on a painted tiger. When the monk asked what power of the staff he had got, why did he not take it out and throw it away before the congregation? Then there would have been a real dragon, a real tiger, calling forth clouds and mists."

Now let me ask, why all this—shall we say—much ado about nothing? If modern Zen is a system, what kind of a system is it? It seems chaotic, and how conflicting are the masters' views! Yet from the Zen point of view there is one current running through all these confusions, and each master is supporting the others in a most emphatic manner. An apparent contradiction in no way hinders the real endorsement. In thus mutually complementing each other, not indeed logically but in a fashion characteristically Zen, we find the life and truth of the *koan*. A dead statement cannot be so productive of results. Hakuin's "one hand", Joshu's "cypress-tree", or the Sixth Patriarch's "original face",[1] are all alive to the very core. Once touch the heart of it and the whole universe will rise from its grave where we have buried it with our logic and analysis.

For the benefit of students who wish to know more about

[1] These are some of the first *koans* for Zen students.

the *koans* which are given to Zen students for solution, a few of them are given here. When Kyosan received a mirror from Yisan, he brought it out before an assemblage of monks and said: "O monks, Yisan has sent here a mirror; shall it be called Yisan's or mine? If you call it mine, how is it that it comes from Yisan? If you call it Yisan's, how do you account for its being in my hands? If you can make a statement that hits the mark, the mirror will be retained; if you cannot, it will be broken in pieces." This he declared three times and as nobody came forward to make a statement the mirror was destroyed.

Tozan came to Ummon for instruction; the latter asked:

"Where do you come from?"

"From Sato."

"Where have you spent the summer?"

"At Hoji of Konan."

"When did you leave there?"

"On the twenty-fifth of the eighth month."

Ummon suddenly raised his voice and said: "I spare you thirty blows. You may now retire."

In the evening Tozan went to Ummon's room and asked what his fault was, so grave as to deserve thirty blows. Said the master, "Is this the way you wander all over the country? O you rice-bag!"

Yisan was having a nap, when Kyosan came in. Hearing the visitor, Yisan turned about toward the wall.

Said Kyosan, "I am your disciple; no formality is needed."

The master made a movement as if he were awakening from sleep; Kyosan started to leave the room, but the master called him back. Said Yisan, "I am going to tell you about my dream."

Kyosan leaned forward as if listening.

Yisan said, "You guess."

Kyosan went out and brought a basin filled with water and a towel. With the water the master washed his face, but before he had resumed his seat another monk, Kyogen, came in. The master said, "We have been performing a miracle—and not a trivial one at that."

Kyogen replied, "I have been below and know all that has been going on between you."

114

"If so, tell me how it is," demanded the master.

Kyogen then brought him a cup of tea.

Yisan remarked: "O you two monks, what intelligent fellows you are! Your wisdom and miraculous deeds indeed surpass those of Sariputra and Maudgalyayana!"

Sekiso (Shih-shuang) died and his followers thought that the head monk ought to succeed him. But Kyuho (Chin-feng), who had been an attendant to the late master, said: "Wait, I have a question, and the successor ought to be able to answer it. The old master used to teach us thus: 'Stop all your hankerings; be like cold ashes and withered plants; keep the mouth tightly closed until mould grows about it; be like pure white linen, thoroughly immaculate; be as cold and dead as a censer in a deserted shrine.' How is this to be understood?"

"This," said the head monk, "illustrates a state of absolute annihilation."

"There, you utterly fail to grasp the meaning."

"Do I? If so, have an incense-stick lighted; if I do not really understand the old master, I shall not be able to enter into a trance before the stick burns up."

So saying, the head monk fell into a state of unconsciousness from which he never arose. Stroking the back of his departed fellow-monk, Kyuho said, "As to getting into a trance you have shown a splendid example, but as to understanding the old master you have just the same significantly failed." This well illustrates the fact that Zen is entirely different from being absorbed in nothingness.

The number of koans is traditionally estimated at 1,700, which, however, is a very generous way of counting them. For all practical purposes, less than ten, or even less than five, or just one may be sufficient to open one's mind to the ultimate truth of Zen. A thoroughgoing enlightenment, however, is attained only through the most self-sacrificing application of the mind, supported by an inflexible faith in the finality of Zen. It is not to be attained by merely climbing up the gradation of the koans one after another, as is usually practised by followers of the Rinzai school. The number really has nothing to do with it; the necessary requirements are faith and personal effort, without which Zen is a mere bubble. Those who regard Zen as speculation and abstraction will never obtain the depths of it, which can be sounded only through the highest will-power. There may be hundreds of *koans*, or there may be an infinite number of them as there are infinite numbers of objects filling up the universe, but it does not necessarily concern us. Only let one gain an all-viewing and entirely satisfying insight into the living actuality of things and the *koans* will take care of themselves.

This is where lurks the danger of the *koan* system. One is apt to consider it as everything in the study of Zen, forgetting the true object of Zen, which is the unfolding of a man's inner life. There are many who have fallen into this pitfall and the inevitable result has been the corruption and decay of Zen. Daiye (Ta-hui) was quite apprehensive of this when he burned up the book on one hundred *koans* which was compiled by his master Yengo (Yuan-wu). These one hundred *koans* were selected from Zen literature by Seccho (Hsueh-ton), who commented on them with verses, one to each. Daiye was a true follower of Zen. He knew well the object which his master had in view when he made remarks upon these selections; he knew very well also that they would subsequently prove a self-murdering weapon against Zen; so he committed them all to the flames.

The book, however, has survived the fire and is still in our possession as one of the most important treatises on Zen; indeed, it is a standard text and authority, to which appeal is still made to settle points of doubt in the study of Zen. The work is known in Japanese as *Hekigan-shu* (*Pi-yen Chi*). To outsiders it is a sealed book; in the first place the Chinese is not after the classical model but is filled with colloquialisms of the T'ang and Sung period, which can now be traced only in Zen literature, while it is most vigorously written. Secondly, the style is peculiar to this kind of work, and its thoughts and expressions seem to be so unexpected as to stagger the reader who expects to find in it ordinary Buddhist nomenclature or at least tame classicalism. Besides these literary difficulties, the *Hekigan* is naturally full of Zen. However, those who want to know how *koans* are handled by Zen followers will do well to consult the book.

There are some other books dealing with the *koans* which are more or less after the style of the *Hekigan*; such are the *Shoyoroku*,

Mumonkwan, *Kwaiankokugo*, etc. In fact, all the Zen writings known as *Goroku* (*Wu-lu*, "sayings and dialogues") as well as the biographical histories of Zen masters, of which we have a large list, treat the *koans* in the way peculiar to Zen. Almost every master of note has left his *Goroku*, which largely constitute what is known as Zen literature. Where the philosophical study of Buddhism abounds with all sorts of annotations and exegeses and analyses which are often very detailed and complicated, Zen offers pithy remarks, epigrammatic suggestions, and ironical comments, which conspicuously contrast with the former. Another characteristic of Zen literature is its partiality to poetry: the *koans* are poetically appreciated or criticized. Of this the *Hekigan-shu* (*Pi-yen Chi*) or *Shoyo-roku* (*T'sung-yung Lu*) are most significant examples. The first is by Seccho, as was already mentioned, and the latter is by Wanshi (Hung-chih), who also poetically comments on a different collection of *koans*. Zen naturally finds its readiest expression in poetry rather than in philosophy because it has more affinity with feeling than with intellect; its poetic predilection is inevitable.

IX

THE MEDITATION HALL AND
THE MONK'S LIFE[1]

THE Meditation Hall (*zendo*) is where Zen educates its monks.
To see how it is regulated is to get a glimpse into the practical
and disciplinary aspect of Zen. It is a unique institution and
most of the main monasteries in Japan of the Zen sect are pro-
vided with it. In the life of the Zen monks in the Meditation
Hall we are reminded of the life of the Sangha in India.

The system was founded by the Chinese Zen master, Hyakujo
(Pai-chang, 720–814), more than one thousand years ago. He
left a famous saying which had been the guiding principle of
his life, "A day of no work is a day of no eating," which is to
say, "No eating without working."[2] When he was thought by
his devoted disciples to be too old to work in the garden, which
had been his favourite occupation, they hid all his garden tools,
as he would not listen to their repeated remonstrances. He
then refused to eat. "No work, no living." At all the Meditation
Halls work, especially that which is commonly regarded as
menial, is the vital element in the life of the monk. It thus
implies a great deal of manual labour, such as sweeping, cleaning,
cooking, fuel-gathering, tilling the farm, or going about begging
in the villages far and near. No work is considered to be beneath
their dignity, and a perfect feeling of brotherhood prevails among
them. They believe in the sanctity of manual work; no matter
how hard or how mean the work may be, they will not shun it,
and they keep themselves in every way they can; for they are
no idlers, as some of the so-called monks or mendicants are, as
for instance in India.

Psychologically considered, this is splendid; for muscular
activity is the best remedy for the dullness of mind which may
grow out of the meditative habit, and Zen is very apt to produce
this undesirable effect. The trouble with most religious recluses

[1] This is fully treated in my recent work entitled *The Training of the Zen
Buddhist Monk*, richly illustrated by Rev. Zenchu Sato, of Kamakura. Also
see *Zen Essays*, I, p. 299 *et seq.*
[2] Cf. Psalm 128: "Thou shalt eat the labour of thine hands; happy shalt
thou be, and it shall be well with thee."

is that their mind and body do not act in unison; their body is always separated from their mind, and the latter from the former; they imagine that there is the body and there is the mind and forget that this separation is merely ideational, and therefore artificial. The aim of the Zen discipline being to annul this most fundamental discrimination, it is always careful to avoid any practice which tends to emphasize the idea of onesidedness. *Satori* in truth consists in reaching the point where all our discriminatory notions are done away with, though this is by no means a state of emptiness. The sluggishness of mind which is so frequently the product of quietistic meditation, we can thus see, is not at all conducive to the maturing of *satori*, and those who want to advance in the study of Zen have naturally to be always on guard in this respect lest it should finally altogether stop the fluidity, as it were, of mental activity. This is at least one reason why Zen followers object to the mere practice of Dhyana. The body kept busy will also keep the mind busy, and therefore fresh, wholesome, and alert.

Morally, any work involving an expenditure of physical force testifies to the soundness of ideas. Especially in Zen is this true; abstract ideas that do not reflect themselves forcibly and efficiently in practical living are regarded as of no value. Conviction must be gained through experience and not through abstraction. Moral assertion ought everywhere to be over and above intellectual judgment; that is, truth ought to be based upon one's living experience. Idle reverie is not their business, insist the followers of Zen. They, of course, sit quietly and practise *zazen*; that must be done if they are to assimilate whatever lessons they have gained while working. But as they are opposed to "chewing the cud" all the time, they put into action whatever reflections they have made during hours of quiet-sitting and thus test their validity in the vital field of actualities. It is my strong conviction that if the Zen monastery did not put faith in working and keeping the blood of the monks circulating, the study of Zen would have sunk into the level of a mere somniferous and trance-inducing system, and all the treasures garnered by the masters in China and Japan would have been cast away as of no more value than heaps of rotten stuff.

The Meditation Hall, or Zendo as it is called in Japan, is a rectangular building of different sizes according to the number of monks to be accommodated. The one at Engakuji, Kamakura, is about 35 × 65 feet and will take in thirty or forty monks. The space allotted to each monk is one *tatami*, or a mat 3 × 6 feet, where he sits, meditates, and sleeps. The bedding for each never exceeds one large wadded quilt about 5 × 6 feet, be it winter or summer. He has no regular pillow except that which is temporarily made out of his own private property. This latter, however, is next to nothing: it consists of a *kesa* (*kasaya*) and *koromo* (priestly robes), a few books, a razor, and a set of bowls, all of which are carried in a papier-maché box about 13 × 10 × 3½ inches. In travelling this box is carried in front, suspended from the neck with a broad sash. His entire property thus moves with its owner. "One dress and one bowl, under a tree and on a stone" graphically describes the monk's life in India. Compared with this, the modern Zen monk must be said to be abundantly supplied. Still his wants are reduced to a minimum and none can fail to lead a simple, perhaps the simplest, life if he models his after the life of a Zen monk. The desire to possess is considered by Buddhism to be one of the worst passions with which mortals are apt to be obsessed. What, in fact, causes so much misery in the world is the universal impulse of acquisition. As power is desired, the strong always tyrannize over the weak; as wealth is coveted, the rich and poor are always crossing swords of bitter enmity. International wars rage, social unrest ever increases, unless this impulse to get and to hold is completely uprooted. Cannot society be reorganized upon an entirely different basis from what we have been used to see from the beginning of history? Cannot we ever hope to stop the massing of wealth and the accumulation of power merely from the desire for individual or national aggrandizement? Despairing of the utter irrationality of human affairs, Buddhist monks have gone to the other extreme and cut themselves off even from reasonable and perfectly innocent enjoyments of life. However, the Zen ideal of putting a monk's belongings into a tiny box is his mute protest, though so far ineffective, against the present order of society.

In India the Bhikshu never eats in the afternoon; he properly eats only once a day; for his breakfast, in the American or

English sense, is no breakfast. The Zen monk is supposed to have no evening meal, but the climatic necessity being impossible to ignore, he has a meal after a fashion, but to ease his conscience he calls it "medicinal food". The breakfast, which is taken very early in the morning while still dark, consists of rice gruel and pickled vegetables. The principal meal is at about ten in the morning and consists of rice (or rice mixed with barley), vegetable soup, and pickles. In the afternoon, at four, they have what was left from dinner, and no special cooking is done. Unless invited out or given an extra treatment at home by some generous patron, their meals are as described above, year in, year out. Poverty and simplicity is their rule.

We ought not, however, to conclude that asceticism is an ideal of life for Zen monks; for as far as the ultimate significance of Zen is concerned, it is neither asceticism nor any other ethical system. If it appears to advocate either the doctrine of suppression or that of detachment, it is merely so on the surface, for Zen as a school of general Buddhism inherits more or less the odium of the Hindu ascetic discipline. The central idea, however, of the monk's life is not to waste but to make the best possible use of things as they are given us, which is also the spirit of Buddhism everywhere. In truth, the intellect, the imagination, and all the other mental faculties as well as the physical objects that surround us, our own bodies not being excepted, are given for the unfolding and enhancing of the highest powers possessed by us, and not merely for the gratification of individual whims and desires, which are sure to conflict with and injure the interests and rights to be asserted by others. These are some of the inner ideas underlying the simplicity and poverty of the monk's life.

At meal-time a gong is struck and the monks come out of the Zendo in procession carrying their own set of bowls to the dining-room, but do not sit until the leader rings a bell. The bowls which each brings are made of wood or paper and are well lacquered; they are usually four or five in number and fit into one another like a nest. The sutra (Hridaya Sutra) and the "five meditations" are recited, and then the monks who are serving as waiters serve the soup and rice. They are now ready to take up their chopsticks, but before they actually partake of their sumptuous dinner, they think of those departed spirits and other beings who are living in this and other worlds, and each taking out about seven grains of rice from his portion offers them to the unseen. While eating perfect quietude prevails; the dishes are handled noiselessly, no word is uttered, no conversation goes on, and all their desires are indicated by folding and rubbing their hands. Eating is a serious affair with them. When another bowl of rice is wanted, the monk holds out his folding hands, the waiter notices it and sits with the rice receptacle before the hungry one; the latter takes up his bowl, lightly passes his hand around the bottom to wipe off whatever dirt may have attached itself and be likely to soil the hand of the waiter. While the bowl is being filled, the eater keeps his hands folded; the rubbing of his palms against each other shows that the waiter has put enough rice or soup in his bowl.

The rule is that each monk should eat up all that is served him, "gathering up the fragments that remain"; for that is their religion. After a third or fourth helping of rice, the meal comes to an end. The leader claps the wooden blocks and the waiters bring hot water; each monk fills his largest bowl with it and in it all the other bowls are neatly washed and wiped with the tiny napkin which is carried by him. Then a wooden pail goes round to receive the slop; each monk gathers up his dishes and wraps them up once more; the tables are now empty as before except for the grains of rice that had been offered at the beginning of the meal to the invisible beings. The wooden blocks are clapped again and the monks leave the room in the same quiet and orderly procession as they entered.

The industry of the monks is proverbial. When the day is not set for study at home, they are generally seen soon after breakfast, about half past five in summer and half past six in winter, out in the monastery grounds or tilling the farm attached to the Zendo. Later, certain groups of them go into the neighbouring villages to beg for rice. They keep the monastery, inside and outside, in perfect order. When we say, "This is like a Zen temple," it means that the place is kept in the neatest possible order. Commonly attached to a Zendo are some patrons whose homes are visited regularly for a supply of rice or vegetables. When begging they will often go out miles away; they may often be seen along a country road pulling a cart loaded with pumpkins or potatoes or daikons. They sometimes go to the woods to gather fuel and kindling. They know something of agriculture, too. As they have to support themselves they are at once farmers, skilled workmen, and unskilled labourers; they often build their own Zendo and other buildings under the direction of an expert. Their labour is not at all perfunctory; they work just as hard as ordinary labourers, perhaps harder, because to work so is their religion.

The monks are a self-governing body; they have their own cooks, proctors, managers, sextons, masters of ceremony, etc. Though the master or teacher of a Zendo is its soul, he is not directly concerned with its government, which is left to the senior members of the community, whose character has been tested through many years of discipline. When the principles of Zen are discussed, one may well marvel at their deep and subtle "metaphysics" and imagine what a serious, pale-faced, head-drooping, and world-forgetting group of people these monks must be; but in their actual life they are very common mortals engaged in menial work. They are cheerful, crack jokes, are ready to help one another, and despise no work which is usually considered low and unworthy of a cultured person. The spirit of Hyakujo is ever manifest here. The faculties of the monks thus receive an all-round development. They receive no formal or literary education, which is gained mostly from books and abstract instructions; but what they do gain is practical and efficient, for the basic principle of the Zendo life is "learning by doing". They disdain soft education and look upon it as a predigested food meant for convalescents. When a lioness gives birth to her cubs it is proverbially believed that after three days she pushes them over a precipice to see if they can climb back to her. Those that fail to meet this test are no longer cared about. Whether this is true or not, something like it is aimed at by the Zen master, who will often treat his monks with every manner of seeming unkindness. The monks often have not enough clothes for comfort, not enough food to satisfy hunger, not enough time to sleep, and, to cap these, they have plenty of work, both menial and spiritual. These outer necessities and inner aspirations, working together upon the character of the monk, often end in producing a fine specimen of humanity called a full-fledged Zen master. This unique system of education, which is still going on in every Rinzai Zendo, is not very well known among the laity, although there is at present the tendency for the latter to get as much information as possible of the life in the Zen monastery. But the merciless tide of modern commercialism and mechanization is rolling all over the East, so that almost no corners are left for a quiet retreat, and before long even this solitary island of Zen may be buried under the waves of sordid materialism. Even the monks themselves are beginning to misunderstand the spirit of the early masters. Though we cannot deny the fact that there are some things in this monastic education which may be improved, its highly religious and reverential spirit toward life and work must be preserved if Zen is to live at all for many years to come.

Theoretically, Zen envelops the whole universe and is not bound by the rule of antithesis. But this is a very slippery ground and there are many who fail to walk upright; and when they tumble the fall is quite disastrous. Like some of the medieval mystics, Zen students sometimes turn into libertines, losing all control of themselves; history is a witness of such, and psychology can readily explain the process of such degeneration. A Zen master once said: "Let a man's ideal rise as high as the crown of Vairochana (highest divinity), but let his life be so full of humility as to be prostrate even at the feet of a baby." The life in a Zen monastery is minutely regulated and all the details are enforced in strict obedience to the above spirit. This is what has saved Zen from sinking to the level of some of the medieval mystics, and it is why the Zendo plays so great a part in the teaching of Zen.

When Tanka (Tan-hsia) of the T'ang dynasty stopped at Yerinji in the Capital, it was severely cold; so taking down one of the Buddha images enshrined there, he made a fire of it and warmed himself. The keeper of the shrine, seeing this, was greatly incensed, and exclaimed:

"How dare you burn my wooden image of the Buddha?"

Tanka began to search in the ashes as if he were looking for something, and said:

"I am gathering the holy *sariras*[1] from the burnt ashes."

"How," said the keeper, "can you get *sariras* from a wooden Buddha?"

Tanka retorted, "If there are no *sariras* to be found in it, may I have the remaining two Buddhas for my fire?"

The shrine-keeper later lost both his eyebrows for remonstrating against this apparent impiety of Tanka, while the Buddha's wrath never fell on the latter.

Though I am doubtful of its historic accuracy, this story is notable and all Zen masters agree as to the spiritual attainments of this Buddha-desecrating Tanka. When a monk once asked his master about Tanka's idea of burning a statue of Buddha, the master replied:

"When cold we sit around the hearth with fire burning."

"When hot we go to the bamboo-grove by the stream."

"Was he then at fault or not?"

Whatever the merit of Tanka from a purely Zen point of view, there is no doubt that such deeds of Tanka are to be regarded as highly sacrilegious and to be avoided by all pious Buddhists. Those who have not yet gained a thorough understanding of Zen may go to all lengths of committing every manner of excess and even crime—this in the name of Zen; and for this reason the regulations of the monastery are very rigid that pride of heart may depart and the cup of humility be drunk to the dregs.

When Shuko (Chu-hung) of the Ming dynasty was writing a book on the ten laudable deeds of a monk, one of those self-assertive fellows came to him, saying:

"What is the use of writing such a book when in Zen there is not even the atom of a thing to be called laudable or not-laudable?"

Shuko answered, "The five aggregates (*skandha*) are entangling, and the four elements (*mahabhuta*) grow rampant, and how can you say there are no evils?"

The monk still insisted, "The four elements are ultimately all empty and the five aggregates have no reality whatever."

[1] *Sarira* (*shari* in J. and *she-li* in C.) literally means the "body", but in Buddhism it is a kind of mineral deposit found in the human body after cremation. The value of such deposits is understood by the Buddhists to correspond to the saintliness of life.

Shuko, giving him a slap in the face, said, "So many are mere learned ones; you are not the real thing yet; give me another answer."

But the monk made no answer and started to go away filled with angry feelings.

"There," said the master smilingly, "why don't you wipe the dirt off your own face?"

In the study of Zen, the power of an all-illuminating insight must go hand in hand with a deep sense of humility and meekness of heart.

There is a period in the monastic life which is exclusively set apart for the mental discipline of the monks, when they are not hampered by any manual labour except such as is absolutely necessary. This period is known as *sesshin*. It takes place a few times, each time lasting a week, in the season known as the "summer sojourn" (*ge-ango*), and again in the one known as the "winter sojourn" (*setsu-ango*). Generally speaking, the summer sojourn begins in April and ends in August, while the winter one begins in October and ends in February. *Sesshin* means "collecting or concentrating the mind". While these *sesshins* last, the monks are confined in the Zendo, get up earlier than usual and sit further into the night. There is a "lecture" (*koza* or *teisho*) every day during the *sesshin*. The textbook used may be any one of the Zen books such as *The Hekiganshu*, *The Rinzairoku*, *The Mumonkwan*, *The Kidoroku*, *The Kwaian-kokugo*, etc. *The Rinzairoku* is a collection of sermons or sayings of the founder of the Rinzai Zen sect. *The Hekiganshu*, as mentioned before, is a collection of one hundred *koans* annotated, expounded, and appreciated. *The Mumonkwan* is also a collection of *koans*, forty-eight in number, with comments peculiar to Zen, and much simpler than the *Hekigan*. *The Kidoroku* contains the sayings, sermons, poems, and other works by Kido (Hsu-t'ang) of the Sung dynasty. He was the teacher of Dai-o Kokushi, whose line of Zen transmission is the one still flourishing in Japan. *The Kwaian-kokugo* is the compilation by Hakuin of Daito Kokushi's sermons and critical commentary verses on some of the old masters. To an ordinary reader these books are a sort of *obscurum per obscurius*. After listening to a series of lectures, the monk may be left in the same lurch as ever unless he has opened an eye to the truth of Zen. This inscrutability is not necessarily caused by the abstruse nature of the books, but because the listener's mind is still encrusted with the hard shell of relative consciousness.

During the *sesshin*, besides the lectures, the monks have what is known as "*sanzen*". To do *sanzen* is to go to the master and present their views on the *koan* they have for the master's critical examination. In the days when a great *sesshin* is not going on, *sanzen* will probably take place twice a day, but during the special time of "thought collection"—which is the meaning of *sesshin*— the monk has to see the master four or five times a day. This seeing the master does not take place openly; the monk is required to go individually to the master's room, where the interview takes place in a most formal and solemn manner. When the monk is about to cross the threshold, he makes three bows, each time prostrating himself on the floor; he now enters the room keeping his hands palm to palm in front of his chest, and when he comes near the master he kneels down and makes still another prostration. This ceremony over, no further worldly considerations are entertained; if necessary from the Zen point of view, even blows may be exchanged. To make manifest the truth of Zen with all sincerity of heart is the sole consideration; everything else receives only subordinate attention. The presentation over, the monk retires from the room with the same elaborate ceremony with which he entered. This exercise may be very trying on the master, for one *sanzen* for thirty monks will occupy more than an hour and a half of most exacting attention.

Absolute confidence is placed in the master so far as his understanding of Zen goes, but if the monk thinks he has sufficient reason for doubting the master's ability he may settle it with him personally at the time of *sanzen*. This presentation of views, therefore, is no idle play for either master or monk. It is, indeed, a most serious affair, and because it is so this discipline of Zen has great moral value. To illustrate this let us consider an incident from the life of Hakuin, the founder of modern Rinzai Zen in Japan.

One summer evening when Hakuin came to present his view to his old master, who was cooling himself on the veranda, the master rudely said, "Stuff and nonsense!" Hakuin repeated loudly, "Stuff and nonsense!" Thereupon the master seized him, boxed his ear, and finally pushed him off the veranda. As it had been raining, poor Hakuin found himself rolling in mud and water. When he recovered himself he returned to the veranda and bowed to the master, who retorted, "O you denizen of the dark cavern!"

Another day, thinking that the master failed to really appreciate the depths of his knowledge of Zen, Hakuin desired to have a settlement with him anyhow. When the time came Hakuin entered the master's room and exhausted all his ingenuity in contest with him, making up his mind this time not to give up an inch of ground. The master was furious, and finally taking hold of Hakuin gave him several slaps and pushed him off the porch. He fell several feet to the foot of a stone wall, where he remained for a while almost senseless. The master looked down at him and laughed heartily; this brought Hakuin back to consciousness, and when he came back to the master he was all in perspiration. The master, however, did not release him yet but stigmatized him as before, "O you denizen of the dark cavern!"

Hakuin grew desperate and thought of leaving the old master altogether, when one day as he was going about begging in the village a certain accident suddenly opened his eye to the truth of Zen, which had hitherto been completely hidden from him. His joy knew no bounds and he came back to the master in a most exalted state of mind. Before he could enter the front gate, the master recognized that something had happened to him and beckoned to him saying: "What good news have you brought home today? Come right in, be quick, quick!" Hakuin then told him all about what he had gone through during the day. The master tenderly stroked him on the back and said, "You have it now; you have it at last!" After this the master never called him names.

Such was the training the father of modern Japanese Zen had to go through. How terribly hard his old master, Shoju, was when he pushed Hakuin over the stone wall! But how motherly he was when his disciple, after so much ill-treatment, finally came out triumphantly! Indeed, there is nothing lukewarm in Zen; if it is lukewarm, it is not Zen. It expects one to penetrate into the very depths of truth, and the truth can never be grasped until, stripped of all trumperies, intellectual or otherwise, one returns to one's own native nakedness. Each slap dealt by Shoju stripped Hakuin of his illusions and insincerities. In fact, we are all living under many casings of illusions and insincerities which really have nothing to do with our inmost Self. To reach this inmost Self, therefore, whereby the disciple gains real knowledge of Zen, the master often resorts to methods seemingly inhuman; indeed, far from being kindhearted to say the least.

In the life of the Zendo there is no fixed period of graduation as in public education. With some, graduation may not take place after twenty years of living there, but with ordinary abilities and a good amount of perseverance and indefatigability a monk is able to probe within a space of ten years into every intricacy of the teachings of Zen. To practise the principles of Zen, however, in every moment of life—that is, to become fully saturated in the spirit of Zen—is another matter. One life may be too short for it; for it is said that even Sakyamuni and Maitreya themselves are yet in the midst of self-training.

To become a perfectly qualified master, a mere understanding of the truth of Zen is not sufficient. He must go through a period which is known as "the long maturing of the sacred womb". The term must have come originally from Taoism; but in Zen nowadays it means, broadly speaking, living a life harmonious with the understanding. Under the direction of a competent master a monk may finally attain to a thorough knowledge of all the mysteries of Zen, but it will be more or less intellectual though in the highest possible sense. The monk's life, in and out, must grow in perfect unison with this attainment. To do this a further self-training is necessary, for what he has gained in the Zendo is after all only the pointing of the finger in the direction where his utmost efforts must further be put forth. But it is no longer imperative for him to remain in the Zendo; on the contrary, his intellectual attainments must be put on trial by coming into actual contact with the world. There are no prescribed rules for this "maturing". Each must act under his own discretion as he meets with the accidental circumstances of life. He may retire into the mountains and live as a solitary hermit, or he may come out into the market and be an active participant in all the affairs of the world. The Sixth Patriarch is said to have lived among the mountaineers for fifteen years after he had left the Fifth Patriarch. He was quite unknown in the world when he first returned to hear a lecture by Inshu (Yin-tsung). Chu (Chung), the national teacher, spent forty years in Nang-yang and never showed himself out in the city. But his holy life became known far and near, and at the earnest request of the Emperor he finally left his hut. Yisan (Kuei-shan) spent several years in the wilderness, living on nuts and befriending monkeys and deer. He was found out, however, and great monasteries were built about his anchorage, and he became the master of one thousand and five hundred monks. Kwanzan, the founder of the great Myoshinji in Kyoto, lived at first a retired life in Mino Province, working for the villagers as a day labourer. Nobody recognized him until one day an accident disclosed his identity and the Court insisted on his founding a monastery in the Capital.

In the beginning of his career Hakuin was the keeper of a deserted temple in Suruga, which was his sole heritage in the world. We can picture to ourselves the extent of its dilapidation when we read this account: "There were no roofs properly speaking, and the stars shone through at night, nor were there any decent floors. It was necessary to have a rain-hat and to wear high *getas* if it rained when anything was going on in the main part of the temple. All the property attached to the temple was in the hands of creditors, and the priestly belongings were mortgaged to the trades-people. . . ."

The history of Zen gives many such examples of great masters who emerged into the world after a period of retirement. The idea is not the practice of asceticism, but is the "maturing", as has been properly designated, of one's moral character. Many serpents and adders are waiting at the porch, and if one fails to trample them down effectively they raise their heads again, and the whole edifice of moral culture built up in vision may collapse even in a day. Antinomianism is also a pitfall for the followers of Zen, against which constant vigil is needed.

In some respects, no doubt, this kind of monastic education that prevails in the Zendo is behind the times; but its guiding principles, such as the simplification of life, restraint of desires, not wasting a moment idly, self-independence, and what they call "secret virtue", are sound for all lands and in all ages. Especially is this true of the concept of "secret virtue", which is a very characteristic feature of Zen discipline. It means not to waste natural resources; it means to make full use, economic and moral, of everything that comes your way; it means to treat yourself and the world in the most appreciative and reverential frame of mind. It particularly means practising goodness without any thought of recognition by others. A child is drowning; I get into the water, and the child is saved. That is all there is to be done in the case; what is done is done. I walk away, I never look backward, and nothing more is thought of it. A cloud passes and the sky is as blue as ever and as broad. Zen calls it "a deed without merit" (anabhogacarya), and compares it to a man's work who tries to fill up a well with snow.

Jesus said, "When thou doest alms, let not thy left hand know what thy right hand doeth; that thine alms may be in secret." This is the "secret virtue" of Buddhism. But when the account goes on to say that "Thy Father who seeth in secret shall recompense thee", we see a deep cleavage between Buddhism and Christianity. As long as there is any thought of anybody, be he God or devil, knowing of our doings and making recompense, Zen would say, "You are not yet one of us." Deeds that are the product of such thought leave "traces" and "shadows". If a spirit is tracing your doings, he will in no time get hold of you and make you account for what you have done; Zen will have none of it. The perfect garment shows no seams, inside and outside; it is one complete piece and nobody can tell where the work began, or how it was woven. In Zen, therefore, no traces of self-conceit or self-glorification are to be left behind even after the doing of good, much less the thought of recompense, even by God.

Resshi (Lieh-tzu), the Chinese philosopher, describes this frame of mind in a most graphic manner:

"I allowed my mind without restraint to think of what it pleased, and my mouth to talk about whatever it pleased; I then forgot whether 'this and not-this' was mine or others', whether the gain or loss was mine or others'; nor did I know whether Lao-shang-shih was my teacher and Pa-kao was my friend. In and out, I was thoroughly transformed; and then it was that the eye became like the ear, and the ear like the nose, and the nose like the mouth; and there was nothing that was not identified. As the mind became concentrated, the form dissolved, the bones and flesh all thawed away; I did not know upon what my frame was supported, or where my feet were treading; I just moved along with the wind, east or west, like a leaf of the tree detached from its stem; I was unconscious whether I was riding on the wind, or the wind riding on me."

This kind of virtue is called by the German mystics "poverty"; and Tauler's definition is, "Absolute poverty is thine when thou canst not remember whether anybody has owed thee or been indebted to thee for anything; just as all things will be forgotten by thee in the last journey of death."

In Christianity we seem to be too conscious of God, though we say that in him we live and move and have our being. Zen wants to have this last trace of God-consciousness, if possible, obliterated. That is why Zen masters advise us not to linger where the Buddha is, and to pass quickly away where he is not. All the training of the monk in the Zendo, in practice as well as in theory, is based on this principle of "meritless deed". Poetically this idea is expressed as follows:

> The bamboo-shadows move over the stone steps
> as if to sweep them, but no dust is stirred;
> The moon is reflected deep in the pool, but the
> water shows no trace of its penetration.

Taking it all in all, Zen is emphatically a matter of personal experience; if anything can be called radically empirical, it is Zen. No amount of reading, no amount of teaching, no amount of contemplation will ever make one a Zen master. Life itself must be grasped in the midst of its flow; to stop it for examination and analysis is to kill it, leaving its cold corpse to be embraced. Therefore, everything in the Meditation Hall and every detail of its disciplinary curriculum is so arranged as to bring this idea into the most efficient prominence. The unique position maintained by the Zen sect among the other Buddhist sects in Japan and China throughout the history of Buddhism in the Far East is no doubt due to the institution known as the Meditation Hall, or Zendo.

INDEX

INDEX

INDEX

Lightning, flashes, 64, 112
Lioness, 123
Lips, the closing of the, 55
Lloyd, Arthur, 42 ff.
Logic, 35, 38, 39, 59, 60, 61, 62, 63, 64,
 66, 67, 68, 69, 99, 113
Logical, 54, 55, 58, 108
Lord's Supper, 39

M

Madhyamika, 31 fn., 36, 49
Madhyamika Sastra, 49
Mahayana, 31, 31 fn., 49, 50, 78, 96
Mahayana pantheism, 108
Mahayana Sastra, 100
Maitreya, 76, 129
Mandala, 36
Manjusri, 55
"Maturing" of moral character, 130
Maudgalyayana, 115
Mayoku (Ma-ku), 85
"Medicinal food", 121
Meditation, 40, 41, 42, 111; quietistic,
 119; the five, 121
"Meritless deed", 132
Middle way, the, 50
Mind (*hsin*), 43, 57, 79, 80, 86, 87; and
 a mirror, 61
Mirror, and Kyozan, 114; the bright,
 48; compared to the mind, 61
Mohammedanism, 40
Mondo, 88
Monotheism, 41
Moon, 74, 78, 106, 132
Mosquito, flying, 54; on an iron bull, 70
Mumonkwan, 117, 126
Myo, 104
Myoshinji, in Kyoto, 130
Mysticism, 32, 34, 35, 36, 44, 45, 75, 111

N

Nagarjuna, 31 fn., 49
Nameless, 61
Nangaku (Nan-yueh), 75
Nansen (Nan-chuan), 53, 70, 71, 93
Nap, Yisan's, 114
Nasti, 50
Naturalism, 86, 87
Negation, 51, 52, 53, 54, 56
Nembutsu, 102 fn.
New Thought, 40
Nihilism, 39, 48, 52, 54, 55
Nine Thoughts on Impurity, 42
Nirvana, 39, 51, 100, 101
"No abiding place", 87, 97
Non-duality, 55, 76
North Star, in the south, 65
Nose, 53, 84, 86, 89, 90, 94, 109, 132
Nothingness, 48, 49, 53, 54, 55

O

Obaku (Huang-po), 52, 93, 94
Old Woman, and the Buddha, 72, 73
One, the, 41, 67, 72, 76; is All, 67

One hand, 59, 109
Original face, 47, 104, 105, 113
Ox, riding on an, 58

P

Pantheism, 41, 67, 78, 79, 106, 107
Pitcher, passing over a, 84
Plank, and stone bridge, 82
Poetry, 117
Poverty, 120, 121, 132
Prajna, 49, 50, 51, 80, 99, 99 fn.
Prajnahridaya, 50, 102 fn., 121
Prajnaparamita, 31
Prajnaparamita-Hridaya Sutra, 50, 102
 fn., 121
Prajnaparamita-Sutra, 49 fn., 86
Psalm, 118 fn.
Pundarika, 101
Pure Land, 56, 110
Purity, absolute, 56

Q

Quietism, 50

R

Raven is black, 52
Reality, 93
Reed, growing through the leg, 77
Reischauer, 42, 43
Religions of Japan, 42
Resshi (Lieh-tzu), 131
Restrictions, 100
Reverie, 119
Rice bag, sitting by the, 73
Richard of St. Victor, 43
Riko (Li-K'u), 70
Rinzai (Lin-chi), 79, 85, 93, 94
Rinzai school of Zen, 102, 111, 115, 124,
 126 127
Rinzairoku, 126
River, thirsty by the, 73
Ryosui (Liang-sui), 85
Ryutan, 89

S

"Sacred Womb", 129
Sakyamuni, 31, 40, 76, 96, 99, 129
Sannyasins, 40
Sandals, Joshu's, 71
Sangha, 52, 118
San-ping, 84 fn.
Sanron, 49
Santi, 50
San-zen, 108, 127
Sariputra, 51, 115
Sarira (Shari, she-li), 125, 125 fn.
Satori, 34, 88 ff., 99, 102, 103, 105, 109,
 111, 119; defined, 88, 95; by Myo,
 104, 105; of Kyogen, 91
Seccho (Hsueh-tou), 116, 117
"Secret Virtue", 131
Seihei (Ch'ing-ping), 73
Sekiso (Shih-shuang), 46, 50 fn., 115

135

9 781434 104762